I Promised
I Would Tell

By Sonia Schreiber Weitz

Edited by Susan Belt Cogley

To Amx,

Sonia

Facing History and Ourselves National Foundation, Inc.
Brookline, Massachusetts

FACING
HISTORY
AND
OURSELVES

Cover: A photograph of the painting "Collective Memory" by artist and Holocaust survivor Samuel Bak.

Facing History and Ourselves
16 Hurd Road, Brookline, MA 02445
(617) 232-1595
www.facinghistory.org

Printed in the United States

ISBN 0-9615841-3-0

Dedicated to my sister Blanca
whose courage and love
willed me to survive,
and to my husband Mark
whose love and understanding
healed my body and soul.

Table of Contents

Poems

Acknowledgements

This book was made possible by many volunteers who devoted many hours of editing and production work.

Management from beginning to end was directed by former Facing History and Ourselves Financial Manager Joe Wiellette.

Sonia spent many hours organizing the book with Margot Stern Strom, executive director of Facing History, and Marc Skvirsky, vice president for program.

Other staff members of Facing History, Program Associates Steve Cohen and Jimmie Jones, contributed editing and production talent.

Major editing was done by Susan Belt Cogley, whose skill and commitment deserve our deepest gratitude and appreciation.

Cover painting courtesy Pucker Gallery, Boston.

Facing History and Ourselves
National Foundation

Facing History and Ourselves is a nonprofit educational organization whose mission is to engage students of diverse backgrounds in an examination of racism, prejudice, and antisemitism in order to promote a more humane and informed citizenry. As the name Facing History and Ourselves implies, the organization helps teachers and their students make the essential connections between history and the moral choices they confront in their own lives by examining the development and lessons of the Holocaust and other examples of genocide. It is a study that helps young people think critically about their own behavior and the effect that their actions have on their community, nation, and the world. It is based on the belief that no classroom should exist in isolation. Facing History programs and materials involve the entire community: students, parents, teachers, civic leaders, and other citizens.

Founded in 1976 in Brookline, Massachusetts, Facing History has evolved from an innovative middle school course to an international organization serving more than 20,000 teachers and an estimated 1.5 million middle and high school students each year in the United States and around the world. Facing History is also constantly expanding its reach through technology, and bringing important lessons about the dangers of prejudice and the power of civic participation to more and more educators and students globally.

Foreword

"The experience lies beyond our reach. Ask any survivor," said Elie Wiesel. "He will tell you; he who has not lived the event will never know it. And he who went through it will not reveal it, not really, not entirely. Between his memory and its reflection there is a wall and it cannot be pierced. The past belongs to the past and the survivor does not recognize himself in the words linking him to it.

"The survivors of the Holocaust who tell their stories bear witness, transmit a spark of the flame, tell a fragment of the tale and remember for those who begged them to tell the story."

Sonia Weitz tells her story. Her memories give a history to mothers, fathers, sisters, brothers, sons, and daughters who were murdered in Europe because they were Jews.

In many ways, Sonia speaks for all survivors. As these witnesses to history are increasingly no longer with us to provide direct testimony, her writing continues to tell the world about the horrors of the past.

There is an irony in the stories of Sonia and of other survivors of the Holocaust which puzzles me deeply. How out of such darkness shines their light, out of such hate comes their love, out of such degradation shows their dignity, out of such despair is their hope?

Sonia is a teacher. She believes that the students and adults she reaches can take a leap into her past and emerge with the courage to care more about their neighbors. She brings new meaning to the saying, "a teacher affects eternity."

Sonia accepts every invitation to reach Facing History teachers and classrooms because she is hopeful and beautiful. This book is another way for her to reach children whom she trusts will make a better world for all. We thank Sonia for her commitment, dedication, and grace.

Margot Stern Strom
Executive Director, Facing History and Ourselves

Preface

As a survivor of the Shoah, I come from another world, a universe where genocide was committed with scientific precision by implementing just three basic ideas:
1. You cannot live among us as Jews . . .
2. You cannot live among us . . .
3. You cannot live . . .

Yes, we struggle to comprehend the unthinkable—an era when death factories were operated by a self-appointed "super race," whose success was enhanced by sympathizers and collaborators from many nations.

I come from an age of darkness when my people— even the children—were condemned to torture and death for no other reason than because they were Jewish. Of course, not all of the victims were Jewish, but *all* the Jews were victims.

The handful who survived try to bear witness; some in silence, which is perhaps the most fitting testimony of all, and some by speaking out. A tragedy of such overwhelming dimension creates an uncommon opportunity to explore, to question, to challenge, and hopefully to learn. Lessons and parallels . . . Learning to be human? Just what have we learned?

The Armenian massacres still make up an historically "forgotten genocide." The Cambodian tragedy is yet another scar upon creation. Then there was Bosnia. . . Rwanda . . . Sudan . . . . These people and countless others all have been victims of prejudice and ignorance, deprived of freedom and dignity. It has been said that after Auschwitz all things are possible. Was, then, the Holocaust a "pilot project" for the destruction of humanity? Or are we to perceive it as an event—unprecedented but not inevitable—whose lessons cannot, must not, be ignored?

Genocide is the end result of hatred, prejudice, ignorance, and indifference. When scapegoating and stereotyping go unchallenged, sooner or later we all become enslaved. Those of us who survived that other universe where the darkness was almost complete have an obligation to warn you, because we know that under the right conditions it can happen again, anywhere, to any people.

We, the survivors of the Holocaust, are the credible link between this world and "the other place." But how does one bear witness to the unspeakable? Some of us try and fail . . . and try again, because we dare not be silent.

Normal standards do not apply to the Holocaust. Even language fails and words like hunger, fear, hot, cold, and pain lose their meaning. In fact, the Holocaust is a crime without a language. Yet we must speak about it, and we must remember from generation to generation, because if we remember, then memory will (we hope) shield us from repeating such unthinkable evil.

Sonia Schreiber Weitz

For *Yom Ha'Shoah*

Come, take this giant leap with me
into the other world . . . the other place
where language fails and imagery defies,
denies man's consciousness . . . and dies
upon the altar of insanity.

Come, take this giant leap with me
into the other world . . . the other place
and trace the eclipse of humanity . . .
where children burned while mankind stood by,
and the universe has yet to learn why
. . . has yet to learn why.

1 *Fragments of Light 1928-1939*

When I was a child, the world was a safe place for me. This is the way it should be for a young boy or girl. But in 1939, when I was only eleven years old, I found out the terrible truth. The world was not a safe place, not if you were Jewish and lived in Europe. In fact, the world was anything but safe. It was a dangerous and cruel place, populated by people bent on the torture and destruction of me, my family, and my people.

My home was in Poland, a country in the central part of Europe. I was born there in the beautiful old city of Kraków in August, 1928. My parents, my sister, and I lived in a modest, but comfortable apartment on Kazimierz in the Jewish section of the city. My mother's name was Adela Finder Schreiber. Like most mothers of that time, she was a housewife dedicated to the care and well-being of her husband and children.

My father, Janek Schreiber, was a middle-class businessman. He had a small shop in Kraków where he sold leather and shoe supplies. To this day I can remember my cousins and me playing games of hide-and-seek on shelves stacked with chunks of tanned leather. Many years later, when I moved to Peabody, Massachusetts, a leather city, the smell of leather was truly haunting.

My sister Blanca is eight years older than I, and even as a child I adored her. I was a chubby little girl with straight hair and an upturned nose that I hated. Blanca, on the other hand, had beautiful curly hair and a straight nose. When Blanca was about

14, she began dating Norbert, a handsome young man who lived down the street near Kraków's Wisla River.

Every day Norbert would carry Blanca's books home from Hebrew High School. From the beginning I loved Norbert, even though he teased me about being a dreamer with my head in the clouds and called me *Pyrek*, or pug nose. I often accompanied Norbert and Blanca as they strolled hand in hand through Kraków's beautiful public gardens. How patient they were to listen to my childish chatter and racing imagination!

Sonia's grandmother with her children. Sonia's mother is in front.

My father and his family were city people—beautiful, sophisticated, and elegant. My mother's family came from the lovely sprawling countryside outside of Kraków. Every summer, my mother would take my sister and me on the long train ride to her family's farm in Rajsko. *Raj* means "Eden" in Polish, and in reality the farm was nothing short of paradise. It was filled with flower gardens, fruit orchards, and lush meadows. There were also horses, cows, chickens, and geese. My grandfather had died when my grandmother was still quite young, so it was she who ran the farm. We all were very proud of our grandmother Rachael.

Summers on the farm were filled with laughter and joy. With so many cousins, I always had lots of children to play with. My uncle Julek, who lived in the next village, would come to visit riding on a pony. Or was it a donkey? Anyway, I remember giggling a lot because his feet dragged in the dirt road. My father came every weekend, and we went on picnics. Once I fell into cow manure, and even after a thorough bathing, no one except my father would come near me. Best of all, I recall the smell of freshly baked bread smothered in homemade plum preserves and the smooth goodness of the buttermilk we drank to wash down my grandmother's delicious scrambled eggs.

My grandmother had a little dog named Aury. He was all white with a black eye patch. How I loved him! Once, when we were leaving the farm at the end of our vacation, Aury tried following our train to Kraków just to be with me. But his legs were too short, and he soon grew tired and gave up. This was fine with my father, who said, "No dogs in the city. Too dangerous."

Was it dangerous for me to have a dog, I wondered, or was the city a dangerous place for a dog? Certainly the city could be a dangerous place. Even as a very young child I knew that. In the 1930s, Kraków had a large Jewish population. Out of the 250,000 people who lived in the city, about 60,000, or one-quarter, were Jewish. In fact, there were many Jewish people throughout Poland and had been since the tenth century. Although over three million Jews lived in Poland at this time, they were seldom treated as equals by their Polish neighbors. This was especially true when Poland faced bad times. When the Polish people suffered, the Jewish people bled.

From my earliest years I remember pogroms, vicious attacks against the Jewish people on the streets of Kraków. As soon as I learned to read, my eyes would confront the ugly letters—"Death to the Jews"—painted on walls and street signs. I think I was only five when I first felt a strange ache in my heart and the sting of tears in my eyes as I listened to my parents' whispers—"They are beating the Jews again."

One incident is especially vivid. My father was being shaved in a barber shop when he heard that some students were attacking Jews in the neighborhood of my school. He ran out of the barbershop and came rushing into my school, right into my classroom. I can still see him. Half of his face was shaved and half was still full of lather. He looked so funny that I laughed and laughed, and he laughed with me. Despite such incidents, I felt safe and protected. I did not believe that anything really bad could ever happen to me or my family.

Yet bad things could happen to us, and my parents knew it. In the early 1930s, they watched fearfully as Adolf Hitler and his Nazi followers unleashed their terrible power in Germany, depriving German Jews of their rights and debasing them as human beings. Then in 1936 my parents' fear turned to disbelief as Hitler strayed beyond German borders and began chipping away at parts of Europe. What would happen when the greedy Nazis turned their sights toward Poland?

I must have been around seven or eight years old when I first overheard the anguished conversations of my parents late at night. Often my Uncle Leon and Aunt Berta would join them. Over and over again, the four adults debated the question of what they ought to do. Should they stay in Poland and pray that the world would stop Hitler? Or should they leave the country? One question led to another. If they left Poland, where could they go?

No place in Europe was safe. The most likely places lay outside Europe. One of these places was Palestine, the ancient homeland of the Jewish people. But for thousands of years, Palestine had been ruled by other people. Now it lay in British hands.

My father, who was a Zionist, and who therefore believed in Jews returning to the land of their origin, argued in favor of Palestine. But how could he leave his father, who was very sick? How could he just pick up his wife and children and move them out of Poland? I remember my mother saying that life in Palestine was very difficult. Besides, the awful truth was that we could not go to Palestine even if we chose to do so. Each time my father mentioned going there, my uncle would softly chide him. "Don't be foolish, Janek," he would say. "Despite the Balfour Declaration, the British no longer support the establishment of a Jewish homeland in Palestine. Now they support the Arabs, and the Arabs do not want any more Jewish people entering the country."

The other place that my family might have chosen was the United States. But here too there was a serious problem. The United States had very strict quotas. These quotas set limits on the number of people who could enter the United States from any given foreign country in any given year. In the 1930s, the total of all quotas was about 154,000 people per year. Of this number, 84,000 were assigned to the British and Irish, people who were not in danger. The quota for all Polish people, both Jews and Christians, was only about 5,000, which meant that 5,000 Christian Poles might fill the Polish quota each year. As my parents worried and waited, the awful truth became apparent. We were considered surplus population. No one in the world wanted us.

On April 28, 1939, my parents' worst fears came true. On that day Hitler stood before the Reichstag (Germany's Parliament), and announced his latest plan. Having already taken over the Rhineland, Austria, and Czechoslovakia, he now announced that the Polish Corridor, a strip of land that lay between Germany and Poland, rightfully belonged to Germany. We all knew that his claims to the Polish Corridor were just the beginning. It was only a matter of time before he invaded Poland.

As Poland prepared to fight, Norbert, along with thousands of other young men, was drafted into the Polish army. Late that summer my family and Norbert's parents went to visit him at the army encampment just outside of Kraków. I remember seeing lots of horses. Now I realize how ridiculous it was that the Polish army hoped to stop Hitler's war machine on horseback. At the time, however, I only remember thinking that war was coming. In the midst of it all, Blanca and Norbert became engaged to be married.

The German invasion of Poland began on September 1, 1939. My father and I were about to enter a pastry shop when suddenly we heard the alert—shrill sirens—warning everyone to take cover. We went to the closest shelter, thinking that it was just another practice drill. But of course, it was not. When we got out of the shelter and made our way home, we realized that Poland and Germany were now at war.

The Germans called their invasion a *Blitzkrieg*, or lightning war. It was like no other attack in history. Wave upon wave of German planes flew overhead as thousands of German tanks and troop trucks crossed the Polish border. Everyone in Poland prayed for help from the outside world, but no help came. Within six days, German tanks rolled into Kraków.

Blanca was beside herself with worry about Norbert. When bombs fell during the first days of the war, she refused to go with us to the air-raid shelter. What if Norbert sent word and she was not at home to receive it?

Miraculously, Norbert did return home. As the defeated Polish army retreated, Norbert managed to escape and hide on a farm where he buried his uniform and documents. He also grate-fully accepted various pieces of female clothing from the farmer's wife. Then he made his way to Kraków by crawling through the underground sewage system. He finally arrived home smelling so bad and looking so awful that his own mother almost turned him away. We all rejoiced with Blanca when Norbert's brother Marcel brought us the wonderful news that Norbert was safe.

The news of Norbert's homecoming was the only bright spot in a dismal, bleak landscape. Each day brought new horrors, new decrees depriving Jews of their rights. It is true that the Poles suffered under German occupation. They too were brutally persecuted by their German captors. But as Jews, we were twice victimized, first by the Nazis and then by many of our Polish neighbors. We became victims of the victims.

Still, life went on. And despite the raging madness, Blanca and Norbert decided to marry. Since more than three Jews were not allowed to gather together, the wedding of my beloved sister took place in hiding in a cellar. The date was November 12, 1939—nine weeks after the Germans had entered Kraków. I remember holding a braided candle to light the ceremony. My hand trembled as I listened for sounds from the street.

Of all of my relatives and loved ones, only Blanca and Norbert survived the Holocaust with me. So the memory of their wedding is bittersweet—the sweetness of hope in the midst of despair and the bitterness of knowing there really was no reason to hope.

In 1964, in honor of Norbert and Blanca's twenty-fifth anniversary, I put my feelings about their secret wedding into words.

Secret Wedding

. . . And so they were wed in a secret place;
A handful of people . . . a damp basement room
No music, no flowers and no pretty lace
For the bride and groom.
Wishing for a bit of time they may borrow,
In a country conquered and plunged into gloom,
Fully aware that a cruel tomorrow
Would come all too soon.
This time their parting—a nightmare to bear!
The kind that awaking wouldn't dispel;
Each of them sentenced in helpless despair
To a private hell.

As an officer in the Polish army and as a Jew, Norbert was twice marked by the Nazis. So Norbert and Blanca began their married life in hiding, which meant they went from one relative to another, from one "safe" house to another. At the beginning my parents urged them to leave Poland and head east with other young Jews toward the Soviet Union. I shudder to recall that my mother and father planned to send me, their little *Soneczka*, along too—because "you have to save the children." But, in the end, Norbert and Blanca decided to stay. And so I was able to remain with my parents. My greatest wish always was to be with my mother, my father, Blanca, and Norbert.

2 *Into Darkness*
1939-1941

Soon 1939 came to an end. The new year brought more restrictions, more humiliations, more acts of violence. The Germans ransacked our homes and took away Jewish property and businesses (often simply handing them over to the Poles). I remember our apartment suddenly being empty because we had to give everything up. I remember the echo in the house.

I can vividly recall my father's reaction when he learned about the first victim in our family—my Uncle Henek. Henek was married to Aunt Sonia, one of my father's younger sisters. Aunt Sonia and Uncle Henek lived not far from us in the town of Rzeszów. Henek was a wealthy man in Rzeszów, a leader in his community.

Uncle Henek was out of town when the Gestapo (the German secret police) came for him. The Gestapo arrested my aunt instead. When Henek learned of her arrest, he hurried back to save her. The Nazis released Sonia, who rushed home to Vitek, their only son. (Both were later killed in the Rzeszów Ghetto.) The Gestapo then sent Henek along with other leaders of Rzeszów to the newly-built Auschwitz, which, in 1940, functioned as a camp for political prisoners. Some weeks later, my Aunt Sonia received her husband's ashes in an urn. My father broke down and sobbed. It was the first time in my life that I had ever seen my father cry. It would not be the last.

Throughout 1940, German soldiers patrolled the streets in search of victims. Sometimes the victims were learned rabbis or Jewish scholars. The Nazis would shave off or tear out the beards of these pious old men and force them to pray out loud, dance, and perform various humiliating acts for the Nazis' entertainment.

Murder of Jews became commonplace. We faced instant death for failure to wear the white band with the blue Star of David on our left arm. I remember embroidering mine. It took hours, but I was very proud of my handiwork. I wanted the band to be a sign of pride, if only to myself.

In April 1940, the Germans declared that by November 1 Kraków had to become a German city which must be rid of its "Jewish element." Jews who wished to remain in the city had to apply for special permission. The authorities issued about 30,000 *Ausweise*, or permits. Jews were constantly required to produce these documents for inspection and were immediately deported if they did not have them.

Many people left Kraków voluntarily in order to avoid forced deportations; others were forcibly deported. I think that it was around this time that my parents took me to nearby

Uncle Henek's only son, Vitek (center) was killed in the Rzeszów Ghetto.

Tarnów, where we had some family. Perhaps my parents felt we would be safer in a small town.

In time, other relatives from Kraków joined us in Tarnów. Among them was Leon, one of my father's four brothers. He came with his wife Berta and their two daughters, Blania and Niusia, both of whom were close to my age. Since they lived near us in Tarnów, my cousins and I became very good friends. We all

10

worried about Uncle Leon, who was sick with tuberculosis. His constant coughing was like a knife in our hearts because we could do nothing to help him.

By now the Nazis were rounding up Jews and shooting them in public squares. Blood flowed in rivers down the streets of Poland's cities, towns, and villages. Tarnów was no exception. Most of my family was killed there, including Leon, his family, and my beloved grandmother Rachael. Another member of my family was hacked to pieces in a public square.

The story of Bronia, my father's youngest sister, is particularly haunting. Bronia was a beautiful girl only about a year older than Blanca. She was married to Willek, a handsome, reckless young man. Somehow they managed to obtain false "Aryan" papers. With these papers, they defied the Nazis in every way possible. They did not wear the mandatory Star of David. And they traveled gaily around Tarnów on bicycles, defying the law that forbade Jews from owning bikes. Eventually someone turned them in. Bronia and Willek were shot and killed on the street.

Another tragic memory involves a friend I had in Tarnów. Her name was Miriam. One day Germans stopped her in the street. They hit her in the mouth, knocking out all her teeth. I remember gazing in horror at her bloody disfigured face. After this, she disappeared, and I never saw her again. For months, maybe years afterward, I had nightmares about all *my* teeth being knocked out.

In reality, I was living a nightmare. Still, I was only twelve years old, and I had a young girl's hopes and dreams. So in the midst of all this killing, I fell in love for the very first time. He was the milkman's son, and I was crazy about him. He had a guitar. I have a very special picture in my mind of him playing his guitar outside my window.

I also had a child's view of the world. I was deeply disturbed and puzzled by my own mother's bewilderment and suffering when my grandmother Rachael was killed. After all, I reasoned, *mamusia* was an adult and I did not think that adults needed their parents. But I was only twelve years old. And I did need my parents. I needed them very much. No matter what happened around me, as long as I had my parents, I felt safe.

In March, 1941, we returned to Kraków. The occasion of our return was no cause for celebration, for we were not allowed to

11

return to our homes. Instead my mother, father, and I—along with thousands of other Jews—were forced into the Kraków Ghetto. Blanca and Norbert came too. Perhaps they felt it was safer to be inside the ghetto than to be in hiding on the outside.

On March 29, 1941, the ghetto was sealed off within a wall topped with a barbed wire fence. German soldiers stood guard at the gates so that no Jew could leave without special permission. The gates leading out were always closed, but the gates leading in remained open. In the following months, the Germans forced thousands of Jews from neighboring communities into the ghetto. The ghetto became so crowded that at one point my parents and I shared a room with three other families. For privacy, we hung blankets from the ceiling. But nothing could keep out the sounds of misery.

Within the walls of this prison, our days were filled with hunger, filth, and disease. Our nights were filled with terror of the unknown. Any moment might bring a fate worse than living in the ghetto and that was the fate of leaving it for an unknown destination.

These forced exits, known as "transports for resettlement," were part of the big lie told to us by the Nazis. "We need your skills; your work is essential. You will be fed, reunited with your family." We heard the lie, but in our heart of hearts we did not believe it. Somehow we knew that those taken from us were being sent to their death.

The old (anyone over fifty), the young (anyone under four-teen), and the sick (those who were physically or mentally handi-capped) went first. Since the magic age for children was fourteen, my parents managed to get me false papers that claimed I was fourteen.

The Nazis rounded up those who had been "selected" and herded them onto cattle cars. Most of us never saw these people again. The words in this poem express how I felt at the time.

Silent Echo

my eyes once gazed
upon eternity
my ears once heard
a silent echo reign
without compassion . . .
love . . . humanity . . .
to dull the pain

3 The Ghetto
1941-1943

I was twelve and a half in March, 1941 when my family was forced into the ghetto. I remained there for two years. During those years, I recorded my thoughts in a diary. I had always liked to write, and in the ghetto I found that writing helped me cope a little better with the horrors around me. I especially liked writing poetry, so I also included poems in my diary.

Although my diary did not survive the war, the memory of what I had experienced and written in the ghetto did not fade. So in 1946, one year after the war ended, I sat down to write about my life in the ghetto. In fact, I tried to reconstruct from memory the original pages of my diary. The following pages contain an English translation of the "reconstructed diary" which I wrote in 1946.

Sonia's mother, Adela Finder Schreiber

15

W marcu 1943 roku zamknięto nas
~~to~~ w obozie koncentracyjnym (K-Z)
Płaszów.

    Trudno się było przyzwyczaić do
wysokiej przeży, do olbrzymiego zimnego
baraku, do gwaru i krzyków, do przekleństw
i płaczu... trudno było stać godzinami
na olbrzymim APEL-placu, a trudniej
jeszcze znosić bicie dnaszych "Panów"...

..Pamiętam zimny dzień księżycowy ...
(Nasz lager trzeba było dopiero budować;
tłuc kamienie, nosić wodę i żwir)...
Wczesnym rankiem zwołano wszystkich
na Apel-plac i wysłano nas do
magazynu po narzędzia do pracy...

A page from Sonia's reconstructed Diary

16

The Diary

April 1941

A month after entering the ghetto, orders came that I had to go to work. One day, other young people and I were piled into a truck and taken out of the ghetto to scrub latrines in the German barracks. At night, as we returned to the ghetto, the soldiers forced us to sing "Roll Out the Barrel" for their amusement. They laughed at the humiliation we faced in singing a cheerful tune after a day of cleaning up their filth. They also laughed because we sang in Polish, a language that the Germans considered inferior.

My mother cried that I had to do this work; she cried bitterly, although she tried to hide it. My father smoked one cigarette after the other. He looked at me with love and pity. He quietly whispered, "That's war. That's the horrible war." I think he felt guilty. The poor man knew that, even in the ghetto, if you had extra money or something of value, it was often possible to find a strong person to work in the place of a child. And so if he had the money, perhaps he could have found a substitute laborer for his beloved little girl. But we barely had money to buy food and no more valuables left. I could see the helplessness in his eyes as I went off to work.

November 1941

One evening, I returned hungry and tired to the house to see my father at the door. He seemed very worried and looked very pale. He asked me to be quiet because my mother was sick. "Sick? How could that be?" I asked. I had never seen my mother sick. No matter how tired or weak, she would always smile, hug me, and say that everything would be all right, that things would get better, that we would be going home soon, that Friday night there would be candles on the white tablecloth again, and that all would be well.

Without making a sound, I tiptoed into the dark room. She was asleep. I lit the small light and came nearer. Her face was burning and her eyes were cloudy. *Mamusiu*, I whispered. I kneeled by her bed and touched her forehead. She gazed at me with a distant look. "My God, she does not know me," I thought. "Her own daughter, and she does not know me."

Later that night, she was taken to the ghetto hospital. She was very sick, suffering from meningitis. Since the hospital was a place for the contagiously ill, none of us were allowed to visit her. But somehow Blanca managed to get extra food and smuggle it in to my mother. My father and I paced endlessly in front of the hospital. Weeks passed in constant fear that the hospital might be evacuated or that the patients might be executed before my mother recovered.

Finally, one day, wrapped in a blanket, my mother came to the window and waved to us. Oh, how good it was to see her! Soon after, she came home, pale and weak. Blanca continued scrounging and somehow was always able to find extra food for our mother.

1942

By the spring of 1942 we had almost no money left. So one day I took the last of our money and went to the bakery for bread. I looked at length at the wonderfully fresh pungent loaves of bread. I faced the baker and breathlessly blurted out a long rehearsed question, "Would you trust me with ten loaves of bread at nine *zloty* each, and I will bring the money tomorrow morning?" The answer came quickly, "Fine."

I could not believe it. I was so proud of myself. I took the ten loaves of bread and ran from one building to another, from one apartment to another, selling each loaf for ten *zloty*. Simple math. Each day I would earn enough money to buy a loaf of bread for my family.

On the evening of the first day, I hid the money under my pillow to protect it until morning. When morning came, I rushed to the bakery and purchased the bread. Slightly embarrassed but happy, I presented the bread to my utterly amazed mother. Unfortunately, this enterprise did not last. Orders came from the Germans to shut down the ghetto bakeries.

Still, we had to have money. So *mamusia* came up with the following plan. In the back of the house in which we lived, there was a garden—once beautiful but now brown and overgrown with weeds. In that little backyard, *mamusia* created a nursery for those children whose lives had been temporarily spared but whose parents were forced into slave labor each day. Many of these parents gladly paid whatever they could to place their children in our care.

It would still be dark when I would get up in the morning and rush from one ghetto house to another, collecting the sleepy-eyed youngsters to bring to our backyard. While my mother cooked and did the laundry, I amused the children with their favorite fairy tales. My imagination was inexhaustible, and in the sunlight I watched their happy smiling faces full of wonderment and hope.

Often, while the children napped, I would sit in the shade of a tree in that dead garden. Enjoying the few precious moments of quiet, I would fill the pages of my diary with my thoughts and feelings. I wrote that I desperately wanted to be good and kind and helpful to my *mamusia*. I wrote also about life—how precious it was and how much I wanted the horrible war to come to an end. In my childish handwriting, I wrote prayers, pleading with God for help. Somehow, I believed He would hear my prayers and answer them. I trusted that the future would be better. In the blessed quiet of these moments, I also wrote poetry.

A Quiet Time

. . . a peaceful moment
to heal my soul
to steady the pounding
within my breast
. . . a quiet time
to make me whole
and let me rest

June 1942

One day in June of our second year in the ghetto, my mother got sick again. This time she refused to go to the hospital. She did not want to waste any time being separated from us. I guess she knew that our time together could be cut short any day. Transports of the old, the sick, and the young were constantly leaving, never to be heard from again.

Each day my father and I carried a cot outdoors for my mother. There, in the shade of my tree, she seemed most comfortable. Often, my father would watch her from afar. He seemed so sad and embarrassed by his helplessness. My heart ached for him, but I knew that I could not approach him and discuss his feelings. He was perhaps more pitiful and bewildered than the rest of us.

Slowly, my mother returned to health. Again, to me, our little nest seemed secure. I began to study in an "underground" school where I met other young people. Education was, of course, forbidden in the ghetto, but there was a group of dedicated Jewish teachers who designed lesson plans for us, giving our young lives a degree of order and defiance.

My new school friends invited me to a "picnic" and I learned to dance. I went for long walks with my friend Rena, who was in love with Bubek, while I was crazy about Jerzyk. Rena and I understood each other.

We were both teenagers, after all.

My parents also insisted that I learn to do something useful. So I became apprenticed to a seamstress. This skill helped me get a job in a German factory called Madrich. Since as a seamstress I was useful to the Germans, I was able to avoid early deportation.

We had a very active resistance movement in the ghetto. As a matter of fact, many of my friends were part of the movement. At one point, I was going to leave the ghetto and join the underground to fight against the Nazis. But, since the Polish partisans rarely accepted Jewish men and women into their units, Jewish resistance fighters faced a tremendous obstacle. We had to change our appearances so that we looked Polish.

My pug nose, which I had always hated so much, was in my favor. But, since most Polish people had fair skin and light hair coloring, my dark hair was a problem. So my mother dyed my hair blond. Then, somehow, she and my father managed to get me the necessary false papers, and I was ready to go.

Unfortunately, the group of youngsters which left just before me was denounced by Poles who collaborated with the Nazis. The Poles turned them in to the Gestapo for the meager reward of a bag of sugar. The Gestapo shot them, one and all. When my parents heard about this act of outrage, they decided that I was to remain in the ghetto.

Still, not all of the Polish people turned against us. For example, the members of one Polish family risked their lives to hide Jadzia, Norbert's niece. As a result of their courage, Jadzia survived the war.

In the meantime, life in the ghetto became "hot." The lists for "resettlement" were growing longer and longer. Without our knowing it, we were condemned to death, but first the Nazis subjected us to unbearable physical and mental tortures.

October 1942

Inevitably, summer turned into fall. By this time, the school we ran was no longer in business. The Nazis had taken all of our children for resettlement. One day in October, I was sitting under my tree writing, when I heard my mother's voice. "Sonia! *Sloneczko!*" (She often called me "Sunshine"). In the window, I could see her silhouette. "Come in, child. It is getting cold outside."

For a moment, I stood at the door and gazed at the dirty blanket that separated one family from another. Then my gaze shifted to my mother. I looked at her as if I were seeing her for the first time. What I saw filled me with shock and surprise. Apparently I had not looked at her closely for a long time. All at once I realized that her hair had turned gray. There were teeth missing in her smile. Her hands were chapped and raw, and her eyes were very, very sad.

That evening, I sat by the window for a long time watching the blood-red sunset. The stars glimmered like pure gold. The moon rose mocking my dreams and hopes. I closed my eyes remembering my childhood through tears. It seemed like a hundred years ago that I had gone to school, played with other children, and looked forward to springtime. How good my life had been. Yet even then, there had been signs of danger all around me. And so I wrote:

How Could We Know

How could we know
What danger signs foretell
We watched the clouds
And heard the thunder near
Until the lightning struck
And darkness fell
But that was yesteryear

22

I was deep in thought about the past and fantasizing about the future when I sensed my mother's hand stroking my hair. By now the room was very cold. We got into bed to keep each other warm. We rested quietly for a long time in this dark dingy room. There was no need for words. I knew that my mother loved me more than her very life. Of course, she loved Blanca as much. She loved Norbert too as if he were her own son. But Blanca and Norbert had each other. And me? In her eyes I was still a child, and she worried desperately about what would happen to me.

Admittedly, I was just an average daughter. I am sure that I could have done many things better. I could have listened more closely. I could have behaved more like a lady. But I did love her deeply. I realized that night what the word "mother" meant to me.

Late that night we were awakened by my father's footsteps. He was very upset. He uttered only two words, "Another transport." I sat up in bed half asleep and looked at him. "Who are they taking this time?" I asked. "Lie down, child," my mother's voice was incredibly calm. "It is God's will."

I cuddled up next to her. We were warm and comfortable. I could feel her heart beating. I held on to her with all my strength. I wanted to feel her next to me. I needed the closeness. I wanted her all to myself. I was afraid that this might be our last embrace, our final chance to be close. I did not dare move. But my eyes were wide open, staring at the dirty gray ceiling. Her arm was across my chest, and I listened to her short uneven breaths.

We waited. Each moment seemed like an eternity. Somewhere a clock struck twelve midnight. Suddenly there were heavy footsteps, and we heard the dreaded pounding on the door. Two men in uniform forced the door open and entered the room. "Adela Schreiber," one voice said. "Get dressed! Immediately!" I froze. My mother sat up on the edge of the bed and slowly started putting on her stockings and her shoes. She put a scarf on her head. "Dress warmly," the voice continued. "You are going on a long journey!"

I ran out into the yard. I screamed into the night, but no

sound came from my lips. The sounds were in my head. I thought I would go mad with grief and rage. I stood there like a stone looking at the sky, cursing the heavens in silence. In reality, the night was quite calm and beautiful. Just an October night in the year 1942. How was it possible that the sky was so peaceful, and where was God?

Suddenly, I found my voice. I cried out, "God, Oh God, Help! How can You let this happen? How can You not be touched by this child whose mother is being taken away by force?"

I trembled as I walked back into the house. I heard doors open and shut and footsteps in the street. "Sonia, Sonia." Now it was my father's voice that pierced the night. "Your mother fainted, and the police have left. For the moment, they are gone. But they will return with a stretcher."

I came into the room. My mother was lying on the floor. Although she had fainted, her eyes were now wide open. Absent-mindedly, she was smoothing out her hair. I heard my father cry, "Oh child, oh child." I came up to him. He was weeping. Something inside of me died. I too wanted to cry but could not. I wanted to speak, to comfort him. I wanted to . . . I do not know what I wanted.

By now, my mother had stood up. Once again, she began getting dressed. Slowly, deliberately, she put on her dress, her sweater, a coat. How carefully she dressed. Calmly and with great care, as if she were getting ready to go to a cinema, she combed her hair. Then she took a bag from the closet. From the cupboard, she took a piece of dry bread and put it into the bag. Dry bread, how terrible! All the time, I stood there, watching her in horror.

Suddenly the door opened, and two men came in with a stretcher. "Where is the sick person?" they asked. Their eyes quickly located my mother. They motioned to the stretcher. "Get on quickly so we can go!" "No, thank you," said my mother in a strange, distant voice. "I am going to make it on my own. No need for the stretcher." Then she added with dignity. "I can walk."

She turned to me. "Come closer, *Sloneczko*," she whispered. I obeyed. She took something from her bag, some money. She put it into my hand. "I know you will need this. It may help." She put her arms around me and whispered, "Remember, I love you." The world was spinning in front of my eyes. As if from afar I heard her last words, "And remember to tell the world!"

"Put an end to this sentimental crap. Enough! Let's go!" yelled the harsh voices. "No, stop, I am going with you," said my father. He went with them, and suddenly I was alone in the night.

Again I called on God for help. I screamed out to the deaf, heartless world. Then, exhausted, I dozed in agony and dreams until I heard my father's voice. "Sonia, child, we saved your mother. Somehow Blanca found out that *mamusia* was on the list. She knew the police must pass by her house on their way to the roundup in the square. So she watched for your mother. Blanca, Norbert, and I managed to create some confusion—a diversion that momentarily caused the police to let go of her. In that split second, we grabbed *mamusia* and hid her in a nearby shed. Then I made a deal with the police. I told them I would go in her place."

I gasped. "Oh, that is nothing," continued my father. "I am a man, and I am strong. I will be fine. The important thing is that your mother is safe." "Safe?" I must be dreaming. "Who said that? It could not be." But my father was standing over me. Suddenly I jumped up and faced him. "No, you are not going! You will not keep your word to the police!"

My father looked at me in bewilderment. I shook him. "Listen! You are not going. Rena's father has connections. He will help later when the *akcja* is over. He will get us whatever papers we need. In the meantime, we will hide together with *mamusia*."

We both rushed to the courtyard. Blanca and Norbert had already been forced to join their work detail. I ran around in panic, looking for Rena's father. When I finally found him, he said that we had done the smart thing. He advised us to hide together. Then, if we survived this *akcja*, he would somehow manage to get us the proper "life" permits.

I hurried back to the courtyard where I saw many members of Norbert's family whispering with my father. The look in my father's eyes told me that there was trouble. "We cannot hide with *mamusia* in the shed," he said. His eyes filled with tears. "The shed is locked, and we cannot find the key." We looked at each other in horror. By now the SS men—those in charge of resettlements and killing—were chasing people to the gathering place, or *Appelplatz*. Their voices taunted us. "*Heraus! Heraus!* Get out, you bastards! This is resettlement. Get out of hiding, you lousy Jews! Get out! Get out!"

The voices were dangerously near. We could not break open the shed door without attracting attention. I sneaked up to the door and whispered, "*Mamusiu,* it's me, Sonia. We cannot open the door. There are too many Germans around. We are going to hide nearby in a cellar. Can you hear me?" "Oh, I would like to be with you," she answered. "We'll be together soon," I promised.

Suddenly I heard shots. There were screams too. My father forced me to move. In the distance, I heard my mother's muffled voice, "Yes, yes, good. Take care of yourself. . ." and the words faded.

We jumped into a basement—my father and I and some other people. We soon realized that Norbert's family was hiding in a cellar next to us. It was dark and damp. Groping, we found some old furniture, and we barricaded the doors and windows. Slowly my eyes became adjusted to the darkness. My father took some crumbs of bread out of his pocket and gave them to me. I ate. I cuddled up next to him. With horror, I listened to the sounds coming from the street. Gunfire . . . One shot after another . . . Terrifying screams, and then quiet and the sound of heavy boots. The blood-curdling screams of children. Those screams surely reached the heavens . . . or did they?

Hours went by. Night passed, and the sun was shining again. We did not respond to the voices from the loudspeakers outside—voices that assured us that we best come out . . . that we would be taken to work . . . that there would be plenty of food and good living conditions. But the voices also warned us that if we did not come out but continued to hide, we would be killed on the spot when they found us.

At some point, I heard a voice, quiet and calm, calling my name. The voice sounded like that of Cyla, Norbert's sister. My father and I looked at each other. "Let's go," I said. "Quiet, we are not going," whispered my father, putting his hand on my mouth.

Again we heard cries and screams. Through the crack in the window, I saw feet, thousands of feet. Some were clad in boots; some in once-elegant high-heeled shoes. Some were marching; others stumbled. Then I saw a tiny foot, a child's foot, tripping on a stone. The little girl, perhaps four years old, cried out as she fell. The next thing I heard was a gunshot. The crying stopped. And then there were more shoes, big and small, in a last silent march before death.

The sun was setting once more. We sensed a terrifying silence, and this time the silence lasted. My father said, "I think it is safe to go out. Let us go and look for your mother." I got up. I was completely paralyzed. My body would not respond, would not move. My father helped me crawl out onto the courtyard. Immediately, we headed for the shed.

By now, I was so numb that the scene before me did not penetrate my consciousness. It was too horrible to confront. The doors to the shed had been ripped open by an ax or a rifle butt. My mother was gone. On the floor lay a crumpled blanket.

My heart sank. If only we had found her body in the shed. If only she had been killed immediately and spared any further suffering. "Oh God, how I wish she had been killed right here. Then I could throw my arms around her and . . . but now there is nothing but emptiness in the shed and in my soul." That night, I wrote:

In Memory To My Mother

Where is your grave?
Where did you die?
Why did you go away?
Why did you leave
Your little girl
That rainy autumn day?

I still can hear
The words you spoke:
"You tell the world, my child."
Your eyes as green
As emeralds
Were quiet and so mild.

You held my hand
Your face was white
And silent like a stone,
You pressed something
Into my palm . . .
And then . . . then you were gone.

I suffered, but
I didn't cry:
The pain so fierce, so deep . . .
It pierced my heart
And squeezed it dry.
And then, I fell asleep.

Asleep in agony
And dreams . . .
A nightmare that was true . . .
I heard the shots,
The screams that came
From us, from me and you.

I promised I would
Tell the world . . .
But where to find the words
To speak of
Innocence and love,
And tell how much it hurts . . .

About those faces
Weak and pale,
Those dizzy eyes around,
And countless lips
That whispered "help"
But never made a sound . . .

To tell about
The loss . . . the grief,
The dread of death and cold,
Of wickedness
And misery . . .
O, No! . . . it can't be told.

Later, the rumors we had been hearing and our worst fears were confirmed, mostly by the underground. I learned that my beautiful mother had been taken to the death camp Belzec. I never saw her again.

My mother's disappearance made me feel old, terribly old. Some people tried to comfort me. Others told me to stop crying, to stop acting like a child. But I could not stop grieving. I remembered how my mother had grieved when her mother had been killed. And so I yelled back that it is right to cry when you lose your *mamusia*. My mother was not a child when her mother was killed. Yet she too cried. Now, like her, I was grown up, and I too could cry if I wanted to.

January 1943

A new year began, and somehow life continued even after my mother was taken away. My father and I became closer than ever. Now he was not only a father to me but a mother as well. I also found great support among my friends, especially Rena. We talked for hours through the long evenings. We shared our feelings and became insepa- rable.

Then I met Adam. Adam was handsome but not very smart. Later, I met Stefan. I immediately fell in love with him because he looked so much like Adam, but he was smarter and more interesting. Stefan would visit my father and me, and apparently father, or *tatus* as I lovingly called him, really liked Stefan too. They played cards and went walking to- gether. And when I was sick, they both worried about me.

And so more weeks and months passed in the ghetto while the war raged on. In silence I prayed, "Oh, dearest *mamusiu*, forgive me for not mourning for you properly. Forgive me for laughing and being joyful. . . ." Besides, in my heart, there was always a spark of hope that the rumors were wrong and that she was still alive.

One day, as I looked around the ghetto, I realized that some of the streets had been blocked off and new walls had been built. In fact, the area had shrunk to less than a third of its original size. By now, thousands of people had been taken away, including Norbert's parents and brothers. Only his sister Cyla was still with us. But later she too would perish.

During the cold days of January and February 1943, the Nazis marched people out of the ghetto and forced them to work on the construction of Plaszów—a new slave labor camp. So we knew that the liquidation, or breakup, of the Kraków Ghetto was imminent. Plaszów was located only two or three kilometers (one and a half miles) from the ghetto. Work progressed quickly.

Every day I confided to my diary the fears about our uncer- tain future, never realizing that these entries would be my very last.

4 *Plaszów*
March 1943-December 1944

On a cold and windy day in March, Blanca and I were among those ordered to leave the ghetto and go to Plaszów. My father and Norbert were also transferred to Plaszów, and I remember rejoicing at our good fortune of not being separated. Although Blanca and I would not be allowed to live with Norbert and my father, at least they would be close by in the men's quarters. And in the meantime, I would have my wonderful sister all to myself.

When we left the Kraków Ghetto for Plaszów, the Germans forced us to leave behind most of our possessions. My precious diary was among those things I was not able to take. Inside the camp, paper and writing tools were forbidden. So I no longer had the comfort of writing down my thoughts, feelings, and poetry. But I was in the habit of expressing how I felt, and I desperately needed to do this. And so I found another way. Instead of putting my experiences on paper, I stored them in my mind. I became a careful observer and recorder of the horror that surrounded me.

When I reconstructed my diary after the war, I also wrote down some of my stored memories of Plaszów. Later I translated them into English. I would like to share these "fragments of darkness" with you now.

Witness To Murder

One cold morning in April, a month after our arrival, we were rounded up and sent to the warehouse for the assignment of equipment. I was in line with Blanca. We were issued two sledge hammers and assigned to work under Beno, a Jewish *Ordnungsdient* (OD), or policeman. Beno took a group of us to a long narrow ditch filled with partially broken stones. Plaszów had been built on two Jewish cemeteries, and the stones had come from the gravestones. He ordered us to use our sledge hammers to break the stones into gravel for a road.

The work was very difficult, making my back ache. My legs and arms were numb. The clothing on my back was soaked with rain and sweat. But Beno was good to us. I clearly remember his kindness. He only ordered us to work when someone in uniform came near—guards or the SS.

Suddenly Beno called out the ominous word *Zex*, the code word for approaching danger. We looked up and saw the arrival of the black limousine that belonged to the dreaded camp commandant Amon Goeth. My sister was working next to me. Next to her was a young woman named Zosia and Zosia's elderly mother.

The car stopped on the hill. As Goeth got out of the car, we saw that he was wearing a white scarf—a sign that this day would claim more victims among us than usual. He approached some women who were carrying water. With a smile, he observed as the women, young and old, trudged bent under the weight of the two buckets that each carried. His demonic eyes focused on an old woman who was carrying only one bucket. The familiar *whoosh* of the whip informed us that he was beating the woman—beating her until she collapsed.

My hands trembled. I concentrated on the sound of the sledge hammer upon the stone—crack, crack, crack—a horrible monotonous sound. Then close by, I heard Beno shout *Achtung*, attention! But Goeth gave another order, "No need to get up! Keep working!" I froze. Blanca whispered in my ear, "Work, Sonia, work." She repeated urgently, "Work. If he should kill me, if he should shoot me, you must be very quiet and keep working. Otherwise, he will kill you as well."

Tears burned my eyes. I thought the unthinkable, "Am I going to lose Blanca? No. No, never! We have to work. Don't think! We have to keep on working. We have to build this road for our new 'home. '" We kept on breaking the stones while above us stood the master of life and death.

Suddenly, without warning, Goeth grabbed the sledge hammer from Zosia's mother. First, he beat her with it. Then he gave her a "lesson" in rock crushing. He took two large rocks and placed a small stone between them. Slowly, methodically, with all of his strength, he hit the rock with the hammer. The blow was too powerful for the hammer. It fell apart in his large inhuman paws. The accident enraged him. He looked around for the nearest target, and his eyes fell once again on Zosia's mother.

As we continued to work, we heard the sounds of his whip beating the woman. We heard her fall. "She fainted?" I asked. "Work," Blanca whispered. "The woman is dead. Do not lift up your eyes. Keep working. "Without lifting my eyes, I could see the fallen woman. Her hands were lifeless. I thought they were stiffening. It was the first time I had ever seen a corpse close up. I had become a witness to murder.

"*Achtung,*" Beno shouted. "The commandant is gone. "I looked around me and saw blood-drained faces and eyes bulging with terror. The only person who was sitting calmly was Zosia. Poor Zosia! She did not even cry. Carefully she put her mother's body in a wheelbarrow and wheeled it calmly up the hill.

Then I heard someone say, "The old woman did not die from the beating. There is a gunshot wound in her head. "In the end, Goeth had shot her with a gun with a silencer. Beno sat down helplessly. There were tears streaming down his face. He bent his head and wept.

"He left. He's gone. The son of a bitch is gone." I heard this all around me, and there was a sigh of relief. But the calm did not last. A few meters in front of us, a woman from another group was pushing a wheelbarrow full of rocks. She moved very, very slowly. She was exhausted. The OD man in her group, seeing that she was about to collapse, took the wheelbarrow from her hands and allowed her to walk alongside. "Oh God, dear God, what if 'he' returns?" I murmured out loud. In fact, the black limousine did appear once more on the hill. But it was too late, too late to warn the OD man who was helping the woman.

Goeth had seen what was going on. He approached. Then without a sound, he beat the OD man brutally and degraded him in a most inhuman way. The woman? He ordered the woman to run, to run in front of him. The woman fell at Goeth's feet and begged for her life. He kicked her away brutally. Then we heard a shot. The woman fell. After a few seconds, she partially raised herself up. We watched as she mutely begged for her life once again. Another shot rang out. This time the woman extended her blood-drenched arms and began dragging herself closer to Goeth's feet. A third shot rang out. This time there was no more movement. The woman was dead, mercifully dead.

My Diary

During our first months at Plaszów, the Germans sent some of us to Kraków to work on cleanup crews in the abandoned ghetto. One of my friends was part of this crew. One day, during her work, she had miraculously come across my beloved diary. That night she bravely smuggled the diary into the camp for me. As she handed the diary to me, others gathered around. They listened as I slowly and deliberately read aloud the memories of my life in the ghetto. Tears streamed down my face and fell on the pages, creating small rivers of blue ink. I read on and on. Soon all of us were crying.

We had a pot-bellied stove in the barracks, and since the evening was cool, a small fire burned in it. When I finished reading my diary, I fanned the fire in the stove. Then, page by page, I fed the record of my young life into the fire. The flames consumed the thin paper, and the letters soared. I knew I had to do this. In this place of inhumanity we were not allowed to have anything that reminded us of being human. Had I been caught with this diary, I—along with many others—could have been killed.

Dancing with My Father

Although men and women lived in separate parts of the camp, the two groups did manage to have contact with each other. For example, on one occasion I was sent to the ghetto with a cleanup detail. While there I found a jacket, a precious warm jacket. I smuggled it back to Plaszów to my father. It was comforting to think that the jacket would keep him warm that winter.

On another day, I sneaked into my father's barracks on the other side of the barbed wire fence. While I was there, I met a boy who was about my age—14 or 15. The boy was playing a harmonica, an offense punishable by death. My father and I listened to the music, and my father said to me, "You and I never had a chance to dance together" . . . and so we danced. It is such a precious image, a bizarre and beautiful gift.

Oil painting by Karen F. Leonard showing Sonia dancing with her father.

Victory

I danced with you that one time only.
How sad you were, how tired, lonely . . .
You knew that they would "take" you soon . . .
So when your bunk-mate played a tune
You whispered: "little one, let us dance,
We may not have another chance."

To grasp this moment . . . sense the mood;
Your arms around me felt so good . . .
The ugly barracks disappeared
There was no hunger . . . and no fear.
Oh what a sight, just you and I,
My lovely father (once big and strong)
And me, a child . . . condemned to die.

I thought: how long
        before the song
                must end

There are no tools
        to measure love
                and only fools

Would fail
        to scale
                your victory

Soon after this, my father and Norbert were taken away on a transport. I never saw my father again.

Life in a Slave Labor Camp

Unlike the major extermination camps (Auschwitz-Birkenau, Belzec, Majdanek, Treblinka, Chelmno, and Sobibor), Plaszów did not have gas chambers or a crematorium. There were, however, mass killings at Plaszów. These killings took place on Hójowa Górka, a hill where the Nazis shot great numbers of people. From the hill, they dumped the victims into a nearby ravine and burned the bodies. The smell of burning flesh never ceased to assault our senses.

There also were medical experiments at the camp and whippings that everyone was forced to watch. The Nazis stripped off the pants of the "guilty" person and then forced him or her to lie across a table. The set number of lashes was twenty-five, but many people, especially those in a weakened condition, passed out after nine or ten. I can still hear their cries of pain and anguish.

At one point the Nazis decided that the Jewish OD men and other Jewish leaders of the camp had outlived their usefulness. So the Nazis rounded them up, moved them to the "hill," and shot them. I remember when the Jewish leadership was killed and burned. I remember the smoke on the hill.

It was at this time that I realized that, since I could not write my thoughts and poems on paper, I would record them in my head. Although everything that happened around me seemed unreal, I concentrated on keeping it real in my head. I often had the feeling that I would one day awaken from this nightmare and come out alive on the other side. Perhaps then I would be able to keep my promise to my mother "to tell the world." Of course, there were other times, grim times, when I felt all was lost. Then, I wanted only to die. But Blanca would not let me. She poked, pushed, and prodded me to stay alive.

Despite the mass killings, Plaszów was primarily a slave labor, not a death, camp. And so our primary function in life was to work for the Nazis. Thanks to my mother, who had made me learn to sew when we were in the ghetto, the Nazis assigned me part of the time to German factories where I helped repair uniforms, shoes, and fur coats.

Sewing was relatively easy work. And occasionally it

provided me and the others in the factory with an opportunity for sabotage (punishable by death). How did we sabotage the Nazis? We sewed sleeves or pant legs together, making it difficult for German soldiers to get dressed. It was a small act of defiance, but it gave us pleasure. Fortunately my sister watched over me, making sure I behaved most of the time.

For part of the time Blanca worked in the bath house where prisoners were sent for delousing. There she managed to cook potatoes and other scraps of food. Often she hid this food behind our bunks. I do not know where she got the extra scraps, but Blanca was always performing miracles, large and small. And so, thanks to her, I often had more to eat than some others at the camp.

After the war Blanca and I argued about whether or not there had been rats in Plaszów. I was adamant that there had been no rats. But Blanca insisted I was wrong. She said, "There were rats because once I hid a quarter of a loaf of bread and when I went to get it, there were chunks missing." In the end, I had to admit it was me. Always hungry, I had located the bread and eaten pieces of it.

The Numbers Had to Tally

By 1943 there were daily transports moving people from Plaszów to other slave labor camps and to extermination centers. My father and Norbert were already gone from Plaszów when my sister and I were placed on a transport. As we sat in grim silence in the cattle car, a small miracle took place. It involved a fellow prisoner, a friend named Fred.

Before coming to the camp, Fred had been a masseur. Goeth, the camp commandant, was very interested in physical fitness, and he chose Fred to be his health advisor. Fred helped Goeth exercise and gave him massages. As a result, Fred became a very privileged person at the camp. He came to know Goeth's assistants and other SS men with whom Goeth had contact.

That day Fred, accompanied by an SS man, happened to pass near the cattle car in which my sister and I had been placed. Fred was always ready to use his influence to help his fellow prisoners, and now he saw an opportunity. The doors to our car had not yet been sealed shut. So Fred looked inside to see who had been selected. When he saw my sister and me, he decided to act. He told the SS man that Blanca and I were essential to the operation of the bath houses, which Fred supervised in addition to his work with Goeth.

Immediately the SS man pointed to us and called, "*Raus!* Out!" We stepped out of the cattle cars and back into life. Fred had saved our lives, but the rest of the people went to their deaths. Among them was my Aunt Syda, one of my father's sisters. I remember looking back at her as I jumped down to the platform.

The Nazis were meticulous record keepers. So they always knew exactly how many people had been placed on each cattle car. Before the doors to each car were sealed shut, they made sure that the numbers tallied. It did not much matter to the Nazis who went, but it did matter that the "numbers" added up correctly.

Since my sister and I had been spared, the count was short by two people. So the Nazis chose two other women to take our places. After the war, I learned that this transport had been taken to Stutthoff, a city in Germany on the Neckar River. All the prisoners had been placed in boats and drowned in the sea.

Regret

Regret is a lonely emotion to bear
Ever more lasting than grief or despair
But burdens of guilt and denial go deeper
For we are indeed our brother's keeper . . .

The Hangings

I don't remember the day. I don't recall the month. I am not even sure what year it was. I remember only that one day we noticed that the Nazis had again erected gallows on the *Appelplatz*. We learned that an old man and a young boy were to be hanged this time.

Is the whole world listening to what I am saying? A child was about to die on the gallows! Why? Because he had committed the terrible crime of singing a Russian song from his childhood.

The Nazis forced all of the prisoners in the camp to watch the execution. The boy was brought forth. He walked with dignity to the gallows. The hangman placed the rope around the boy's neck and pulled. For a moment, the boy hung suspended in the air, and then miraculously the rope broke. The boy fell to the ground still alive.

Perhaps in another universe, at another time, the boy's life would have been spared. Perhaps at another time the executioners would have seen the hand of God in the boy's reprieve. But here, in this world, no such thoughts occurred to the Germans. For the crime of singing a song, the boy must be hanged. He must be hanged again.

And so once more, this slim youngster stood on the scaffold, high up in the clouds. This time he spoke, "I am glad to be dying. Why suffer any further? I am the only one left in my family. I am alone in the world. Why live? For whom? For what? There is no one left who cares about me." Then his words were lost in the wind.

After a few minutes, they dragged out the old man. Moments before, he had tried to commit suicide by cutting the veins in his arms. The old man was all but dead. The hangman had to prop him up on the gallows. But the old man was too weak to stand, even with help. He swayed and fell.

The SS men went crazy with rage. How dare the old man cheat them out of an execution! How dare he take his own life! "Dead or alive, he hangs!" came the orders. And so they managed to prop up the old man once again just long enough to place the rope around his neck. A split second later, his body joined that of the boy, swinging in the clouds.

We were not allowed to leave the *Appelplatz* after the execution. Instead, the Nazis forced us to march around the gallows observing the "lessons of disobedience." As we marched, the camp band played, and the Nazis laughed at the spectacle.

In 1969, more than twenty-five years after the hangings at Plaszów, news cameras showed images of Jews being hanged in a public square in Baghdad, Iraq. Those images at once triggered the memory of the hangings I had been forced to watch in Plaszów. Once again I felt the terror, pain, and inhumanity. And so I turned to my poetry for comfort and wrote this poem.

From Plaszów To Baghdad

In the ancient city of Baghdad
(once the cradle of civilization)
Jews are hanging 'pon the gallows
In a public square.
A blood-thirsty mob
Soon gathers and cheers
And the Jews are dead.

Did you ever bear witness
To a public hanging?
I did.
I remember well
The suspended bodies,
Especially that of the boy
Not yet fully grown —
And of course, the old man
Oh, that old man
Dangling . . .

And the band was playing
(I can hear it now)
Brassy and so very loud,
But not loud enough
To drown out the sound
Of their final heartbeats.

Ashen were the faces
Forced to look upon the gallows,
Upon the convulsed remains
Swinging in the bloody sunset
Limp and grotesque . . .
Dead but not yet useless,
Not to our tormentors;
For them the fun had just begun
And we, the starved, the frozen
Remnants of humanity . . .
We were ordered to march
Eyes to the gallows, single file,
To the music, to the laughter,
To the Nazis' merriment;
For their amusement
We marched.

Oh, it took forever;
The sun disappeared
And the stars came out
And still we marched . . .
We stumbled and fell
And we prayed for death
But the march went on,
Till upon my soul
A picture was wrought
Not to be erased
Ever . . .

Later that night
Our masters tired
And we were dismissed,
It was all over . . .
Except for the smell
Of burning flesh
And the smoke on the hill
That still lingers on
And on . . . in my mind,
In my heart,
In my very soul . . .
Forever.

Many years have passed
But much has not changed.
Still the bloody sun
Glares undisturbed
'pon this callous planet . . .
This world that really
Doesn't give a damn,
This human race;
Just a bit embarrassed
And a little sad . . .
Quickly turning
To something less upsetting,
More pleasant,
More trivial . . .

Giza

I had a friend in Plaszów whom I had known since
Tarnów. Her name was Giza. Giza had always been full of
life. In Tarnów, when she was a sophisticated thirteen and I
a childish eleven, she spent hours in the hallway of our
apartment house trying to teach me to dance. She also
showed me how to fix my hair so that I would look older.
No matter what she did, she always made me feel good
about myself.

Giza did not lose her love of life in the camp, and
somehow she also managed to keep her good looks. As a
result, the Nazis chose her for a special job. On certain days
she was called from our barracks and taken to the house of
the commandant to do heavy housework before dinner
parties and other social affairs.

One night, I remember waiting anxiously for her return.
It was late, very late. For hours I worried that something
terrible had happened to her. And yet I also smiled in
greedy anticipation. Giza sometimes returned from these
parties with stolen scraps of delicacies which she shared with
all of us.

As the hours passed, others in my barracks began to

worry too. "Something must have happened to her," said Mania. "It must be way past midnight." The woman on the bunk above me awoke and began to complain, "Come on, kids, go to sleep! We have to get up at dawn. Don't worry. Giza can take care of herself. You know that the parties at the commandant's house go on all night. She is probably just working and eating when no one is watching."

"No, No!" I interrupted. "They only use the prisoners to do the dirty work before the guests arrive. Giza is always back early. Something must have happened to her."

"Shut your mouth or I'll shut it for you!" yelled the *Kapo* (a higher-level prisoner in charge of barracks and workgangs) from her privileged space at the far corner of the barracks. We grumbled but quieted down.

A few minutes later the door opened, and there was Giza. For a brief moment, her pretty face appeared bathed in the light of the full moon. Her black eyes sparkled with fire, full of mischief as always. Her small body slid soundlessly along the wall. She climbed onto the bunk next to me and with great ceremony unwrapped a bundle of food. What a sight! A piece of apple, a hard boiled egg, some cheese. We devoured every morsel and looked expectantly at her.

"Well, tell us, tell us. What did you do? What happened? Who was the guest of honor?" Giza laughed and held up her hands, "Hold it. I'll tell you, I'll tell you. We worked like the slaves that we are—scrubbing floors and carrying crates packed with vodka, beer, and wine. But then, you won't believe this. Here, Giza lowered her voice and in a most conspiratorial tone continued.

"The chief housekeeper pointed to me and yelled: 'You! Come here. *Schnell!*' She made me take off my dirty smelly clothes, even my shoes. Then she handed me a black dress, a white apron, black shoes and ordered me to wash myself in the basement sink and dress quickly. You should have seen me! I glanced in the hall mirror and couldn't believe my eyes. I looked like a young woman again. I felt like a free person. Even the apron was beautiful!

"The housekeeper looked me over and sneered: 'You'll have to do.' Then she showed me how to carry a tray into the salon where people were laughing and drinking, as they

44

awaited the arrival of an honored guest. Just as I put down a heavy tray, the doors opened wide and the guest of honor appeared. Over and over again, I heard his name repeated as the guests greeted him. The guest was Adolf Eichmann [the infamous SS commander whose job it was to organize the destruction of European Jewry].

"I backed off toward the stairway, afraid to breathe. Commandant Goeth welcomed Eichmann with great pomp and began to present the other SS officers to the guest. I watched, fascinated, as heels clicked and heads bowed—as the smartly dressed ladies offered their bejeweled hands which were quickly grasped and kissed by Eichmann. I stared in horrid fascination."

Giza stopped for a moment and checked to make sure that we were properly impressed by her tale before continuing. "Suddenly I had this crazy idea that I thought I could get away with. Quickly I took off my apron, threw my head back, and stood proud and tall. Then I calmly watched as Eichmann approached me. When he stood in front of me, I modestly lowered my gaze and smiled. He took my hand in his and raised it to his lips and kissed it. Then he looked up and whispered, *Enchantez*."

I gasped, "No! You did not." "Oh, yes, I did," Giza replied. "I tricked him into kissing the hand of a Jewess." Giza's laughter was so contagious that we all joined her. It was not often that we had an occasion to laugh.

We were so preoccupied with laughing that we did not hear the door burst open as two SS men marched into our barracks. We jumped off our bunks and scrambled to attention, as we had been trained to do. But they hardly noticed. They spoke to the Kapo who pointed in our direction. Then they marched straight to Giza. Without a word, they seized her under the arms and dragged her outside. The doors shut behind them, and a moment later we heard a single shot.

Oh, my sweet, brave friend, I screamed soundlessly. My lovely, caring, daring friend, so young and pretty, so innocent and generous. My dear friend Giza, may you rest in peace.

The End of Plaszów

In March, 1944, the Nazis rounded up the Hungarian Jews and dispersed them to slave labor camps and extermination centers throughout Europe. As the Hungarian Jews flowed into Plaszów, conditions in the camp grew very bad. Overcrowding led to more disease and less food. And it seemed as though the Nazis were more anxious than ever to kill anyone they found unfit to live. I remember a doctor who would come in the middle of the night dressed in a black cape like the angel of death. He carried with him a hypodermic needle. There was a woman in my barracks who hiccuped. He gave her a shot and killed her.

Sometime in the summer of 1944, the Nazis began work on the breakup of the camp. At the same time they started transferring prisoners to other camps or extermination centers. In September, as the Soviet army moved into Poland from the East, the Nazis tried to wipe out all traces of the horrendous crimes they had committed at Plaszów.

In December, 1944, when orders came to abandon Plaszów, those of us who were still alive (about 600) made preparations for the forced march to Auschwitz. For weeks we had been hoarding food and searching the camp for discarded clothing. Now we covered our emaciated bodies with layers of rags and stuffed food into our pockets. Finally orders came to leave. Thus ended one year and nine months of our imprisonment in Plaszów.

The fragments of memory which I wrote down in 1946 end here with our expulsion from Plaszów in December, 1944. Although we did not know it at the time, the worst was yet to come.

5 *Auschwitz and Beyond January 1945*

Auschwitz, the largest Nazi concentration and extermination camp, was located near the town of Oswiecim, Poland, about 37 miles west of Kraków. Built in 1940, it originally functioned as a camp for political prisoners. However, its function and capacity expanded in March of 1942 when the Nazis added a second, much larger section of the camp. This was called Auschwitz II or Birkenau. The gas chambers and crematoria of the Auschwitz killing center operated in Birkenau.

In nearby Monowitz, Poland, the Nazis established a third camp—Auschwitz III, also called Buna-Monowitz. Auschwitz III was a forced-labor camp. Its inmates, chiefly Jews, were literally worked to death. Above the main gate of Auschwitz I, a large inscription mocked all who entered. The inscription read: *"Arbeit macht frei."* (Work will set you free.) The inscription was a farce. In Auschwitz, work, if you were chosen for it, meant only one thing—a slow and horrible death.

In December, 1944, just as we were beginning our march to Auschwitz, the Nazis dismantled the technical installations of the gas chambers and crematoria. Although these instruments of death were no longer in working order when we arrived at Auschwitz, the killing did not stop. The Nazis simply reverted to other, less efficient, methods of murder—beatings, whippings, slave labor, shootings, and hangings.

Auschwitz—say the word silently to yourself. Whisper it, if you dare. Say it out loud, if you can. Even today, the mere mention of Auschwitz—the name, the word—conjures up images of darkness, burning, death, and destruction. In Plaszów my sister and I had heard rumors about Auschwitz, but we still clung to

47

the big lie—that we were being "resettled" there to work for the German Reich. Of course, deep inside, Blanca and I knew this was not the truth, but how could we go on if we listened to the nagging voice of truth? And so we lied to ourselves. We lied to stay alive.

I can still remember the "walk" to Auschwitz. Years later I commented that Auschwitz was within walking distance of Plaszów. Nobody understood what that really meant, except for Blanca. Our march took us through the streets of Kraków. It was almost Christmas time and brutally cold. I remember that everything was bright. People saw us, but nobody offered help. Some averted their eyes. Others stared through us as though we were not there. Perhaps, in a sense, we were not there. We were no longer in the land of the living.

How can I describe Auschwitz to those who have not been there? Once again, language fails me. People from every part of Nazi-occupied Europe arrived in cattle cars. The trains pulled in at the railway platform in Birkenau. Brutal guards and SS men with vicious dogs forced the prisoners to leave the cars in a great hurry. Insults, swearing, screams, and endless humiliations assaulted and dulled our senses. *"Schnell! Schnell!"* They shouted. "Quickly. Quickly. Move. Move. Form two lines, men and women separately."

The lines passed before SS officers who were conducting the *Selektion*, directing to one side those unfit for work and to the other side, those who still had some life in them for forced labor. Everybody was screaming in anguish.

Behind the barbed wire, male inmates added their voices to ours. Desperate to have news of their loved ones, they shouted out the names of parents, children, brothers, and sisters. They did this with every new transport that entered the camp. Some of these men threw pieces of bread over the barbed wire, and we grabbed for the food. Their cries of longing and our screams of terror formed a chorus of inhuman sounds that filled the universe. But no one heard those awful sounds, except for us. I know this is true because no one answered. We had been abandoned by the world.

It was very cold when we arrived at Auschwitz—cold and wet. I do not clearly remember the sequence of events, but Blanca and I must have passed through the first selection. I do know that we were taken to the camp's showers to be deloused. After delousing, Blanca and I were placed in line to have our heads shaved and our left arms tattooed with numbers—our "new names." But on this particular day, the day we arrived, the usual Nazi efficiency had broken down. There were too many of us and too few head shavers and tattooists. So Blanca and I don't have a number tattoo, and our hair was never shaved.

We were not in Auschwitz for long. As I have said, Germany was losing the war by this time, and the Soviet army was mounting an offensive in the direction of Kraków and Auschwitz. So in January 1945 the Nazis began evacuating the Auschwitz camps. Approximately 58,000 prisoners were driven from Auschwitz to be sent into Germany and Austria, where the death factories remained temporarily out of reach of the Allies. My sister and I were among the walking dead who were evacuated and forced on the now legendary death march.

Years later, I learned that ten days after we left Auschwitz the Soviets reached the camp. Only a few days and we would have been saved. But this was not to be our fate. We would not escape so easily. Instead we marched, and we marched. In my head, I composed poetry.

Death March

A night . . . A storm . . .
Their blood still warm,
soaking into the snow.
Their bodies recoil
upon frozen soil,
oblivious to the flow
of pain, that whips.
Their lifeless lips
belie this final hell.
At the break of dawn
they barely moan,
a silent: *"Sh'mah—Israel."*

The weather was very cold, and it snowed almost every day. We were dressed in flimsy rags and given no food or water. So we lived on snow and whatever we could scrounge from the earth—roots and rotten potatoes left in the fields.

The ground beneath us was slippery with ice. Many people slipped and fell and could not get up again. Others collapsed from exhaustion. Having no use for these pathetic souls, Nazi guards unceremoniously kicked the fallen bodies into ditches that lay along the side of the road. Every day we saw more bodies. We prayed that our lives would end quickly with a bullet instead of having to die in the ditches.

One night we slept in a hay shed. It was so wonderful to be warm. I removed my soaked shoes. Oh, what a mistake! When the time came to put my shoes back on, my feet were so frostbitten and swollen that my shoes no longer fit. So Blanca ripped the soles from the uppers and used rags to tie the shoes to my stiff, bleeding feet.

Most of the guards rode on horseback. We only rested when they were tired or too drunk to move. Then we would fall down wherever we were. I would not want to get up again. But Blanca would not let me die in the snow. When the march would begin again, she would force me to my feet. At the time, I hated her for that. I wanted only to rest.

Another night, the guards let some of us sleep in an abandoned factory. We climbed up to the floor beneath the roof and collapsed in exhaustion. When it was time to move on, we heard the frightful whistles and shouts of the guards. *"Raus! Raus! Get going! Move!"* We ran outside. The other prisoners were not there. While we had slept, they had marched on. And so the entire column was far ahead of us. We did not know what to do—how to catch up. Our guards saw our bewilderment. They said, "Look, there's only a handful of you. If you want to stay here and hide, go ahead. We'll let you."

I wanted desperately to stay. Throughout our ordeal, I had been consumed by the desire to escape, to hide, to rest, to be left alone. But my sister did not trust the guards. So she grabbed my arm and pulled me in the direction of the column. I moved like a robot, too numb to fight her. Some of the others chose to stay behind. As we raced ahead, I looked back at them with longing. Then we heard the shots. The guards had killed them all. Trusting was punishable by death.

One cold and windy morning as we began yet another torturous day, the guards seemed less watchful than usual. So a small group of women slipped away in search of food. We saw them by the side of the road, clawing at the ground to get at some potatoes or turnips that lay buried beneath the snow. I sneaked up to see if I too might get "lucky," but I simply could not penetrate this mass of starving humanity.

Suddenly I heard a familiar female voice. Startled, I searched out the source of the voice. It belonged to the mother of Romek, a boy from the ghetto who had been in Plaszów with us. I had good news to tell his mother. Romek had been alive when we had left Plaszów. In fact, he may even be among the countless victims on this march.

Hastily, I ran to her. By the time I reached her, I was trembling. I grabbed her shoulders and shook her yelling "Don't you know me? I am Sonia, Romek's friend." She looked at me with a blank stare of madness. "Listen to me," I insisted. "Don't you want to hear what happened to your son, your son Romek, your only son?"

She shrugged and shook me off as if I were a strange insect. Her voice was shrill and hoarse as it emerged through broken teeth and cracked lips. "Get away from me," she screamed. "Get away, or I will tear you to pieces or choke you to death."

She hissed and lashed out at me, kicking the other women at the same time. Her legs were swollen to almost twice the size of her body. Her feet were bleeding through the dirty rags. In her hands she clutched some unidentifiable scraps of food. I backed off and ran. I thought, "Was she but a looking glass of my own image? Is this what the camps did to people?" A thought hit me, and I shuddered. "How dehumanized can we become? Is there no limit to the depth of our misery?"

A cold chill ran up and down my spine as I considered the unthinkable. Had my beloved mother become like this woman, or had they killed her before she became an animal? At that moment I hoped with all my heart that she had been killed soon after entering Belzec. I convinced myself that this was true. There was a twisted kind of satisfaction in that belief. I ate some snow and marched on.

One day, I noticed that my gloves were missing. "Blanca will kill me," I thought. Fred, our friend in Plaszów, had given me those gloves to protect my hands. Now I had lost them. Or perhaps someone had stolen them. I wept, and my tears soaked into the snow. I watched the snow melt and freeze again. I munched on the ice and cried. I cried for my mother, for me, for Blanca, for all of us. But most of all, I cried for my lost gloves.

I sat down hoping that Blanca would not notice. But Blanca noticed as she always did. She pulled me to my feet and rubbed my hands till they felt less numb. Then we continued to drag each other along the slippery road.

After many days the guards located a freight train with cattle cars. Our marching came to an end. The cattle cars had no roofs, and soon we were covered with a blanket of snow. What a picture that created—invisible bodies hidden beneath undulating waves of snow. Surprisingly, the snow insulated us from the cold, providing us with some measure of warmth.

In the cattle cars we were given no daily rations. So the snow was our only sustenance. We ate the snow and let it melt in our precious metal cups so that we could drink it. When we crossed into Czechoslovakia, there were some people—farmers—who risked their lives to approach the cattle cars. They threw to us little bags of potatoes and salt. For awhile, we lived on that.

Wanting to honor these people, I later wrote:

The Righteous Gentiles

There, where the darkness was almost complete,
our spirit defeated and crushed . . .
A human cargo of twisted limbs rushed
toward slaughter. Without food or water;
in transport trains, in freezing rains —
forgotten, alone — except for the few
who simply cared, who somehow dared
come close enough to help a Jew . . .

These were Christian peasants
　　　　who sometimes would throw
　　　　　　　　bags of raw potatoes

Into cattle cars
　　　　through the iron bars
　　　　　　　　of hopeless despair . . .

Finally the train reached Germany. In Germany, the guards
kept stopping the train, looking for a place to unload us. But
every camp was full. In the end, we were accepted at Bergen-
Belsen.

6 Bergen-Belsen and Venusberg
February-April, 1945

For Blanca and me, Bergen-Belsen was much worse than Auschwitz. The guards dumped three hundred of us in a barracks that had room for about fifty people. We had no blankets, no bunks, no food, no space, no latrines. It was the perfect breeding ground for typhus and other diseases that thrive in unsanitary conditions.

Everybody in Bergen-Belsen had typhus. Soon our barracks became infested. Every day the *Kapos* would come into our quarters to dispose of the dead. Sometimes they disposed of those who were still living. There was a fine line between life and death in that barracks. Often we ourselves did not know to which world we belonged.

I remember other things about Bergen-Belsen. I remember the newcomers. Yes, even at this late date the Nazis were rounding up Jews from all over Europe and sending them to the camps. We, the experienced survivors, recognized the newcomers instantly. It was not difficult to do so. The newcomers looked healthy. They had hair. They wore street clothes—the clothes they had on when they had been rounded up. They were still in the land of the living.

I remember hearing their languages and listening to their songs. Many sang songs of longing for their homelands and their families. The Italian girls sang *Mama* in their native language. It was heart wrenching, because we knew they would soon be dead. They did not have our experience—our expertise in surviving.

You might wonder what expertise there was in surviving. In fact, there were many lessons to learn. For example, as experienced survivors we knew that the best position for roll calls was in the middle—out of reach of SS guns and whips, yet close to other victims who might hold you up if you fainted. For food, we knew that the best position was also in the middle of the line. Those in the front often received the watery substance at the top of the bucket. At the end, there might not be any food left at all. No, it was in the middle of the line that one had the best chance of getting some nourishment. The newcomers knew none of these secrets. And so, over time, we watched them die—of longing, of terror, of torture, of starvation.

One night a few of us sneaked behind the German quarters to scavenge for food. I was thinking how brave I was. But I was not brave. I was desperate. And desperation often leads to recklessness. Had we been caught, we would have been shot.

I have already mentioned one of the most dreaded horrors in every camp—the *appell,* or roll call. Roll calls were not new to us. We had lived through them in Plaszów and Auschwitz. Now, once again, we were forced to endure endless hours of standing motionless at attention while the guards counted us. If the numbers did not tally, they counted again and again until the camp commander was satisfied that every prisoner had been accounted for. Clad in rags, we had no protection from ice, wind, or snow. We were weak, hungry, and terribly sick. But standing in fives, we held each other up.

In Bergen-Belsen we had no work. How strange that having no labor added to our nightmare. Our "work," as terrible as it had been in the other places, had defined us. It had placed us in the world of the living. But in Bergen-Belsen we did not work. We rotted. For endless days and nights we crouched, cold and hungry, on the damp floor of our barracks. Crouching was the only position that allowed us some small measure of space. When we were not crouching, we were standing in line waiting to be counted again and again on the *Appelplatz.* Bergen-Belsen was a nightmare of the living dead.

Numb beyond pain, I fantasized. Often, to escape reality, I wrote poems in my head.

Icicles

The wind is brutal, the rain icy-cold.
I shiver and hold out my empty fists,
My stomach twists with hollow cramps. . .
The hunger—not unbearable,
It dulls my wits and sets the mind a-swim . . .
My vision dims, most pleasantly,
I tremble, I weep, and quite detached
I watch myself. Am I asleep?
Or do I now belong among the dead?

And yet I know I am alive, I know
Because along my bony cheek
A tear escapes, it quickly turns to ice —
How nice, how nice to remember . . . to see,
I see — icicles . . . and me:
A little girl, a window sill,
And frost upon the pane . . .
(and down the lane, a friend)
My mother's voice, the smell of food,
My father's laughter fills the air.
I sigh, I stare . . . the wind has chased
My dream away and left but emptiness.
The icicles now burn my lips,
They turn to salt—It's true,
There are no "bitter tears,"
'Cause tears . . . and blood . . . sweat too . . .
They all taste salty, tart—
And bitterness? Ah, bitterness,
That dwells within my heart.

I am cold, hungry, I hurt . . .
Does anyone know I am here?
Does anyone care?

After we had been in Bergen-Belsen for several weeks, we heard that a transport would be leaving for another camp, a labor camp. We desperately wanted to be on that transport. By this time Blanca was sick with typhus. We all knew that the SS would not accept typhus victims on the transport. So Blanca willed herself to appear well so that she could hide her illness from the guards. Miraculously, she passed the selection along with me and about 30 other women.

Very few people survived Bergen-Belsen. So this transport probably saved our lives. On the other hand, had we remained in Bergen-Belsen and had we been able to survive for just a little longer, we would have been set free by the British. There were so many "could have beens," so many "what ifs." These tricks of fate haunt all Holocaust survivors because survival was nothing but dumb luck, pure and simple.

When we got in the cattle cars, I realized that my sister might be dying. At this time, I was sixteen and a half, but age had no meaning in this other world. I was both old beyond my years and much younger. When I realized that I might lose Blanca, I wept in fear. How could I survive without her? She was my lifeline, my savior, my mother, my father, my sister, my family. And I loved her beyond words.

Fortunately, I had others to help me—Selma, Lola, and Edzia. It was not easy to form friendships in the camps, but somehow these three women, Blanca, and I had done just that—become friends. We believed that there was strength in numbers, and so we looked after each other. These three women helped save Blanca's life.

The box cars were so packed with transports from other camps that people literally had to lie on top of each other, stacked like cans on a shelf. But it is impossible for people to exist like this without suffocating. So there was bedlam in the cars—screaming, shoving, prodding, pushing, beating. A new kind of hell descended upon us.

Blanca was too weak to protect herself. So Selma held Blanca's head on her lap, and I tried to shrink—to become invisible so that my sister could have some of my space.

Time does not heal all wounds. Years have dulled the pain but not the memory. Even today I can picture these endless hours with awesome clarity. It is raining and very, very cold. Although the boxcars are sealed shut, the rain leaks through cracks. My sister is moaning softly; the fever and typhus have given her an other-worldly expression, almost peaceful. She hardly moves.

Someone whimpers. Someone dies. I am soaked with helpless perspiration and fear. Panic grips my heart, and I start to shake. "Don't let her die. O God, don't let her die. (God? What God?) Well, I can't just sit here and let her die. Maybe a prayer would help." I wondered how long it had been since I had said the *Sh'mah,* the sacred, ancient chant of the Jewish people that pro-claims the oneness of God.

Then I think, "That is why she is dying, because I have not prayed, because I cannot pray." But another inner voice answers back. "Nonsense! The universe does not work that way. You know this to be true because in the ghetto you prayed and prayed for your mother's life. And your prayers were not answered. They took her from you anyway."

Lola and Selma are trying to give my dying sister a bit of extra space—space so she can lean back. They are pushing a raving old woman aside. The woman screams. Selma puts my sister's upper body on her lap and rocks her back and forth. I squeeze my bones aside to ease her legs down. "How many weeping, whimpering, miserable bodies are there in this dark and smelly pit of hell?"

I lean over and whisper, *"Blaneczko,* can you hear me?" But someone's bony elbow (or was it a knee?) shoves me hard, all the way to the sealed door, near the loathsome can that functions as our latrine. There, in the puddles of urine from the overflowing bucket, I think I am laughing until I notice tears flowing down my cheeks. The sobs make me cough and choke and choke and cough some more, until someone swears at me and threatens to wring my neck if I don't shut up. I swallow the tears and the phlegm. I choke on the bitterness, and I taste the hopelessness of despair.

Over and over again, I repeat, "Don't let her die!" But the wheels of the train have their own refrain. "Die, die," they say. Rain pours down the side of the wall, and I am soaked. Someone touches my arm gently. I tremble. It is Mama Friedrich. She is the mother of Ruth, a girl my own age. Like Blanca, Ruth is also dying of typhus.

Mama Friedrich has a piece of blanket—a threadbare, filthy, lice-infested treasure. All night she has been comforting her daughter, fighting off the other skeletal apparitions like a lioness, like a mother. Now, she stares at me with a sense of pity in her watery eyes which hardly focus. There, in the bowels of dehumanized evil, she takes a piece of this blanket off her own delirious child and wraps it around me.

I shall always remember this human embrace— this act of unbelievable kindness, a gesture of unselfish caring. There, in the very depths of insanity, for one precious moment, this woman of valor, the mother of Ruth, melted away some of my horror.

After several days we reached our destination—Venusberg, a small slave labor camp. In Venusberg we had food and work. We knew by then that if you ate and worked, your chances of survival were better. But in Venusberg, typhus was the killer—the night stalker. And it was stalking my sister.

The first time we had to stand for roll call on the *Appelplatz*, I was sure Blanca was going to die. She was shaking from fever and chills. To add to her misery, she had severe diarrhea. We had to hold her up. One of us had a turtleneck sweater. We stuffed Blanca's legs into the arms of the sweater to keep her warm. Unspeakable memories.

We did our best to help each other. During roll calls the sick could not stand at attention. In fact, most of us could barely stand at all. Heads bent, arms limp, we slumped and swayed from side to side trying to maintain our balance. When the SS guards approached, we would manage to prop each other up until the guards moved on. Then we would resume our slumping positions, temporarily saved until the end of the inspection.

Here, as elsewhere, we hoarded food. Those of us who were sick and could not eat hid the bread in the upper bunks. We had SS women guarding us at that time, and they were crueler than the men. I worry that I am being sexist when I say that I expected the women to be kinder. But I did expect this, and they were not.

During my years in the camps, I had been emotionally tormented, starved, worked almost to death, but I had never been beaten—never until Venusberg. I was in line for our meager daily rations—watery, slimy soup in which some indistinguishable scraps floated. When I got my portion, I gave it to Blanca because she was too ill to stand in line. Then I got in line again and the SS woman, damn her, recognized me. How she could ever recognize one prisoner from the other I'll never know, but she did. Her face became engorged with rage, and she beat me, first with a whip across my back and then with her hand across my face.

The SS women who guarded us in Venusberg were so utterly inhuman that we no longer feared death. We feared life instead.

Cry Children, Cry

Cry to your gods, so they may deliver
Your wretched souls! In the snow a-shiver
Those naked bodies with faces gray,
With lips that forgot how to curse or pray.

Cry children, cry to your gods, be bold!
Your executioner's feet may be cold . . .
They say she is "human," just doing her job,
Perhaps she'll be angered by your muffled sob . .
She may swear and fix her sadistic stare
'pon your rotting bones, exposed . . . bare.

There is no pity! And the ground is frozen!
Yet, if you're lucky, you may be chosen
To rate a bullet, painless and fast . . .
But, no! Your tormentor turned in disgust.

How merciful, had she let you die . . .
Cry children, cry!

One day a fellow prisoner squealed on us. Desperate to earn extra food or relief from work, she told the *Kapo* in charge of our barracks about the bread we had been hoarding. The SS women came that day, climbed up on our bunks, and took away our treasure. But later on, there was also joy for us or perhaps some morbid satisfaction in their action. When they climbed onto our bunks, they became contaminated with typhus. Even they were not immune from the pallor of death that filled the camp.

I remember one friend there. Her name was Erna. Erna was married just before or as the war broke out. She was very much in love with her husband and did not know if he was still alive. But she hoped and prayed that he was. And for Erna, as for many of

61

us, that hope—the hope of one day seeing our loved ones—
sustained her, gave her the strength to go on.

But Erna's hope took a strange twist. She became obsessed
with how she looked. She had been a young, beautiful woman
when she had married. Now, she was emaciated, covered with
boils and scabs. Her once beautiful hair was gone, ravaged by
disease. Her face was that of an old woman.

She prayed that her husband was still alive, but she also
feared seeing him again. Would he still love her, want her, desire
her, cherish her? So almost every night she performed a morbid
ritual. She would remove her scraps of clothing and study her
naked body. She would look at herself and scream that her
husband would never love her—that he would never desire her
again. I don't know if she ever met her husband again. However,
I did find out that she survived the camps. She survived only to
be killed in a streetcar accident after the war.

Perhaps because I was in Venusberg during the last part of
the war, or perhaps because I was older then and more in touch
with what was going on, I have many memories of that camp. I
remember that we had coffee there, or more accurately, a liquid
that resembled coffee. We pooled our coffee and washed whatever hair we had in it. The warm coffee felt good on our heads.

After our hair wash, we would pick through each others'
scalps hunting for lice. And whenever possible, we would turn
our clothing inside out and scrape the infested seams. I catego-
rized the lice. The ones with a big red spot on their backs were the
carriers of typhus. We were especially watchful for those. Hunting for lice became our main spare time activity—our recreation.
Not that we had much spare time.

I also remember the work we did in Venusberg. We built
airplanes for the German Reich at a nearby *Messershmidt* factory.
In order to get to the factory, we had to leave the camp. It was a
long, long march. Being outside the camp was eerie. It reminded
us that another world existed. My work details in other camps
had almost always been inside.

In Venusberg, we worked two shifts, either the morning shift
from 6 a.m. to 6 p.m. or the night shift from 6 p.m. to 6 a.m.
During both shifts we passed homes along the way. In the morn-
ings we would see lights coming on and smoke curling up
through a chimney. The smoke did not mean that bodies were

being burned. It meant that a mother was lighting a fire in the stove to prepare breakfast. We also heard children playing with their dogs. To me, dogs symbolized death because Nazi guards used dogs to rip inmates to pieces. But here there were sweet dogs, dogs like Aury from my grandmother's farm. It was amazing to hear children playing in freedom with their dogs.

My sister was sick most of the time—not able to work. Luckily, though, she was not put on the sick list. Instead she stayed in the barracks while the rest of us went off to work. One time she was so sick that I faked illness to stay with her. I was really afraid that she would die that day, and I wanted to be with her.

This lie almost cost me both my teeth and my appendix. Venusberg was a "civilized camp." This meant that a doctor and a dentist visited once a month. Without question, anybody who was on the sick list would get her appendix removed and teeth pulled. So I had to get myself off the list. Somehow I faked that I was dead. After all, it was not that difficult to do. I certainly looked dead. Blanca eventually did get better. I don't know how that was possible given the conditions in which we lived.

Among the workers at the factory there were prisoners of war—Allied soldiers who had been captured by the Nazis. The soldiers whispered that Allied forces were nearing Germany— that Germany would soon be defeated. Of course, we were not allowed to speak to them directly, but there was always a grapevine, always some method of getting information.

Allied bombings confirmed the rumors, but somehow we never worried about the bombs. During the few bombings that I remember, the Nazi guards and SS officers would hide in shelters. But the prisoners would stand in the open praying that a bomb would fall close by, just to know that somebody cared. The bombs usually fell quite a distance from the camp. Had the Allies only bombed the camps or the railroad tracks along with German factories, the death machine would have been slowed or stopped.

The bombings gave me hope, but my hope soon turned to despair. I came down with typhus and ended up in the sick barracks. It must have been March by this time. The doctor and dentist had stopped coming. The sick barracks was now a quarantine place to separate those with typhus from other prisoners who could still work. Periodically the guards emptied these wards. I'm not sure what happened to these people. I suspect they were killed.

When I was in the sick barracks, Selma, one of our army of five, came and brought me soup. She was a German Jew who had been thrown out of Germany and dumped on the Polish border. Later she had been rounded up with Polish Jews and sent to the camps. Her German was excellent, and she managed to get an extra bowl of soup for me by helping a *Kapo* clean the floors. I'll never forget that.

A Gift Of Life

To Selma, a friend who remained
Human and caring even when night
Descended upon her childhood
And the years of horror,
Of unspeakable evil
All but consumed her very life . . .
And yet, even in that darkness
There were moments of light
(rare and incredible)
And you created for me,
One such memory;
In that "other world"
You brought me food.
Remember, how sick I was
With typhus, fever . . .
You scrubbed the barracks' floors
And the *Kapo* rewarded you
With a bowl of soup . . .
You must have been hungry too,
You were so skinny; a little girl
With great big eyes . . .
But you didn't eat.
Instead, you sneaked into
The crowded, smelly, disease-ridden
"Ward for the sick" and you brought me
A gift of life . . .

One day in April, orders came to evacuate Venusberg. The war was almost over, but not for us. The Nazi obsession to kill all Jews never weakened. So they were evacuating Venusberg to take us to yet another camp—a camp still beyond the reach of the Allied forces. My sister found out about the evacuation and came running from work to rescue me. Somehow she had learned that the sick were not going to be evacuated. So Blanca, with her usual ingenuity, entered the sick ward through a window or hole in the wall. Once again, she saved my life.

Typhus brings on high fever, stupor, dehydration, and delirium. I was so thirsty and exhausted that I could hardly lift my legs. But my three friends and Blanca were there to help me. They took turns, two on each side of me, propping me up and propelling me along toward the train. Somehow they got me on the cattle cars with the others.

Each sealed car contained from 120 to 140 women. There was no air, and I was burning with fever. Every few days, the guards would open the doors to remove the dead. But the dead and the living looked alike, and the guards were not concerned with making the right choices. So Blanca did everything she could to make me appear alive. She would prop me up against the back of the wall and pinch my cheeks to give them some color. Each time, I would pass the selection.

Cattle Cars

Herded together in the burning sun,
the box-car sealed and standing still
on a hill . . . at the end of the world.
Once I was hungry—last night, last year?
Once I knew no fear . . . once there were no trains,
now I dream of rains and tropical fruit,
my throat is on fire. How long has it been—
how long since I've seen my sister?
Panic grips my heart and I start to shake . . .
There she is, *Blaneczka*, alive, awake,
she touches my brow and cries,
someone whimpers . . . someone dies.

I smile and my lips crack. I am happy, but why?
I forget, I sigh—so hard to recall;
the ghetto . . . the wall . . . and my mother gone.
Perhaps she is dead and resting in peace.
I hope she was spared these indignities,
my lovely *Mateczka*—no, I couldn't bear
to watch her shrink and fade away —
like Romek's mother; ugly and mad,
the shaven head, the greedy eyes —
so utterly dehumanized . . .
But God is merciful — He is!
Did He not spare my mother this?
These years of agony and pain,
or is God insane—like me?

My sister—my keeper, whispers in my ear:
"Be quiet, my dear, this is a selection"
yet despite the action—I grin:
"I win, I win." My mother is dead
but instead of tears, I laugh and rejoice . . .

Oh the choiceless-choices we learned to embrace
. . . in that other world . . . in that other place,
where children burned while mankind stood by
. . . and the universe has yet to learn why,
has yet to learn why.

———————————————

After sixteen days in the cattle cars, we arrived at Mauthausen in Austria. Little did I know at the time that Mauthausen was the camp to which both Norbert and my father had been sent in the summer of 1944.

7 *Mauthausen May 1945*

It was in Mauthausen that our nightmare finally came to an end. But not immediately. I remember that when we arrived at Mauthausen we had to climb a large hill to get from the train to the camp itself. Marching up that hill was really above and beyond what we were capable of. In our group of five, Edzia and I were still very sick with typhus. So the other three had to drag the two of us up that hill. I say "had to" because if you were unable to climb that hill, SS guards threw you into wagons heaped with bodies—some dead, some still alive.

Once we navigated the hill and reached the camp, there was no place to go, no place to sleep. Filled to overflowing, the camp was in total disorder. I remember black and green uniforms. There were so many levels of prisoners. And, of course, the Jews were at the lowest level.

Mostly I remember praying that they would let us go to the latrines. We had such diarrhea and vomiting! We were constantly throwing up on each other. My sister was just dragging herself around, trying to keep me alive. I think another day or two would have been too late for me.

And then it happened. Much later, I found out the date—May 4, 1945. Blanca came yelling to tell me that the *Kapos*, guards, and SS had disappeared. The next day, May 5, at 11:30 a.m., American army tanks entered Mauthausen. The prisoners themselves opened the gates to the camp and let the Americans in. And it was over!

The American soldiers were speechless with horror when they saw us. Although Allied leaders and high-ranking military officials had known about the death camps as early as 1942, the soldiers themselves knew very little. So these young soldiers came upon the camps totally unprepared. They entered this unimaginable world and were forever transformed by the atrocities that had been committed there.

I especially remember the expression on the face of one African-American soldier when he saw me. Sick with typhus and fever, unable to distinguish between nightmare and reality, I gazed into his horror-filled eyes.

My Black Messiah

A black GI stood by the door
(I never saw a black before)
He'll set me free before I die,
I thought, he must be the Messiah.

A black Messiah came for me . . .
He stared with eyes that didn't see,
He never heard a single word
Which hung absurd upon my tongue.

And then he simply froze in place
The shock, the horror on his face,
He didn't weep, he didn't cry
But deep within his gentle eyes
. . . A flood of devastating pain,
his innocence forever slain.

For me, with yet another dawn
I found my black Messiah gone
And on we went our separate ways
For many years without a trace.

But there's a special bond we share
Which has grown strong because we dare
To live, to hope, to smile . . . and yet
We vow *not ever to forget.*

The Americans found most of us close to death. So they put together a makeshift hospital in Mauthausen and moved us in.

For Blanca and me, our greatest fear had always been separation from each other—for work, for showers, for anything. It was a tragedy to be separated even for one hour, because we never knew if we would find each other again. As a result, even now with the war over, Blanca would not allow them to separate us. So in order to be near me in the hospital, she claimed that she had some nursing experience. It really did not matter much because the Americans were desperate for help and asked very few questions.

Painting by Sonia just after The Reverand Doctor Martin Luther King, Jr., was killed.

Despite medical attention, thousands of survivors died within days and weeks of liberation. My own life hung in the balance. Almost 17 years old, I weighed only 60 pounds. My hair fell out in clumps. I was so emaciated that the only vein they could find to feed me intravenously was under my knee. As a result, I had to lie on my stomach. But this was very uncomfortable because of my hip bones. They were so pronounced that they dug into the mattress. I remember trying to carve out little holes in the mat-

69

tress in which to place my hips. That's how Norbert found me.

Like Blanca and me, Norbert had been freed from Mauthausen on May 5. Although he too suffered from malnutrition and disease, he had no intention of hanging around to be nursed. Instead, he, along with several other survivors including the now-famous Nazi-hunter Simon Wiesenthal, located an abandoned farm house near Linz, Austria (Hitler's birthplace). There they created Camp Hart.

Camp Hart became one of many displaced persons' (DP) camps established in Germany and Austria after the war. A displaced person is someone who has been uprooted from his or her home. A displaced person is someone with no place to go. In 1945 we, the survivors of the Holocaust, were people without a country, state, or nation. We were *Statenloss*, without citizenship.

Camp Hart, along with other DP camps, also functioned as a documentation center—a place where people could register to find family and friends. Norbert had never given up hope of finding Blanca and me. So at Camp Hart, he asked each survivor who passed through the camp if he or she had news of us. Finally, someone told him that a transport of women had arrived at Mauthausen in late April.

Norbert did not hesitate a minute. He and his friend Nathan appropriated some clean clothes from a farmer's clothesline. They also "borrowed" a car and drove from Camp Hart to Mauthausen.

When Norbert and Nathan arrived at Mauthausen headquarters, they inquired about Blanca and me. The Americans tracked Blanca down at the hospital and sent for her. The reunion was truly a miracle. American soldiers wept as they watched this tender moment.

The Reunion—A Miracle

The fruits of destruction spread through the haze,
When the war finally ended that spring—
Wearing prison garb they searched in a daze,
Like birds without wings . . .
But then a miracle came to unfold
And a momentous reunion took place:
Their eyes bespoke all the words untold
. . . In a mute embrace.

But my father, what of him? Norbert told us that Janek Schreiber, my sweet, gentle father, had been killed weeks before the end of the war. He was killed not by a Nazi but by a Ukrainian *Kapo* who, angered that my father had been unable to work on one particular day, had beaten him unconscious with a chair. Out of all the stories, all the information that Norbert told us, this was the one cold fact, the single piece of information that my mind could process. Later I learned in terrifying detail that, after the savage beating, the *Kapo* had thrown my father into a barrel of water just to make sure he was really dead.

Sonia's fingerprint from Mauthausen. This was signed with Blanca's married name ("cheating" so that we could stay together).

In Memory To My Father

Did the suffering
Drive you wild?
Did you think of me
Your child,
Did you cry?
I know, you'd rather
Spare me the gory truth . . .
Oh, father!

No, the details
Matter not!
But, dear God
You forgot
A man who wept . . .
And begged for life,
Not for himself—
But for his wife . . .

You saw a father's
Tear-stained face,
But showed no mercy!
Not a trace
Of compassion . . .
You watched the pain,
'till his brothers
Were all slain . . .

And still my faith
In You is great,
And still I trust You—
Without hate;
For when he prayed
His dying word:
To save his daughters
—You heard!

8 Displaced Persons Camps 1945-1948

Norbert wanted to take us out of Mauthausen the same day he found us. But he faced some real difficulties getting permission from the authorities to move us. The Americans felt that I was much too sick to leave the hospital. They wanted assurances that I would be under medical supervision.

Blanca refused to leave without me, and Norbert would not leave without her. So the officers in charge cut through the red tape and broke some rules. They phoned the military headquarters in Linz and located a doctor attached to a medical unit. They arranged for him to see me at Camp Hart the next day.

Norbert picked me up like a baby and put me in the back seat of the car. I vomited all the way to Linz. By the time we arrived at Camp Hart, someone had prepared a room for us. My bed was near the window, and there were birds singing in the trees. The room was quiet and peaceful and clean. I could not believe that this was reality. In the camps we used to talk and dream about having a real home, about dying of natural causes in a real bed. Now I wondered, was I going to die?

The first person who came to see me at Camp Hart was Niusiek Strahl. Like Blanca and me, Niusiek was a survivor of many camps. More important, he was a dentist and thus had some medical knowledge. He agreed to take care of me until the doctor arrived.

The first order of business was delousing. All survivors of the camps had to be deloused. But when Niusiek began the procedure, he nearly fainted—not because of how I looked but because of who I was. His family and my family had lived in the same apartment complex before the war. Now we were neighbors again at Camp Hart. Niusiek continued to nurse me when the doctor was not available. He carried out the doctor's orders to give me vitamin shots and take blood tests.

Despite such care, I remained in critical condition through June. In fact, one night, I became so violently ill that Niusiek and Norbert left the camp to get help. But they did not get far. A violent rainstorm stranded them outside of Linz. Fallen trees blocked their exit. Blanca spent the long night watching me slip away and worrying about the fate of her husband and friend. They, in turn, spent the long night wondering if I would be alive in the morning.

Some hospital care was available in the area, but Blanca, Norbert, and I decided that I would not go to a hospital. We still feared hospitals. Our experience over the past six years had taught us that hospitals were places of no return. And so we refused to let them move me to some strange place from which, we were convinced, I would never return. Luckily my doctor, Major Greenspan, agreed to let me stay in Camp Hart and be treated there. Within a month or two, I began to recover.

During my recovery, Norbert and Niusiek would carry me outdoors into the fresh air and place me gently on a mattress. Blanca would serve me wonderful fruit drinks, just like the ones I had fantasized about in the camps. Only these drinks were real. I even had a radio, and for the first time in six years I could listen to music.

Oh, that radio! An American soldier named Joe had given it to us. He was of Italian descent and spoke Italian in addition to English. But he did not understand a word of German, Yiddish, or Polish. And we, of course, knew no English or Italian. Somehow, however, we managed to communicate with him. He was so touched by the miracle of Blanca's and Norbert's reunion that he gave Norbert his own wedding ring, Norbert, in turn, put the ring on Blanca's finger. (She treasures this ring to this day). Joe and other kind and thoughtful American soldiers never opened a package from home without sharing their gifts with us.

One afternoon, resting outside, watching birds in flight and wildflowers swaying in the summer breeze, I let my mind wander and my imagination soar. That day I began the reconstruction of my diary.

74

Soon I also began to write poetry again. Although the rabbis had told us not to recite the *Kaddish*, the Hebrew prayer for the dead, because there was still hope that our loved ones were alive, I knew in my heart of hearts that my mother was dead. I knew I would never see her again. And so I wrote:

Jahr—Zeit
(For my mother)

Through cloudy skies, she's looking down;
A furrowed brow, an anxious frown . . .
Her love still warm, below her breast,
Her broken heart won't let her rest,
With anguish . . . only a mother would know,
When torn from her child, before it has grown.
The clouds will soon pass, so she may find,
The little girl she left behind . . .
She had such hopes for her, such dreams—
The years to give, so few! It seems
They fluttered by like a gentle dove . . .
But she bequeathed a wealth of love,
Of hope, of truth, of will to live
In such a little time to give . . .

(So helplessly she departed,
When my life had barely started)

I was not alone in mourning my losses. In time we all began to mourn the enormity of our personal tragedies. Eyewitness accounts of murdered mothers, fathers, husbands, wives, daughters, sons, brothers, and sisters filtered through Camp Hart. The agony grew unbearable. Each day brought news of still another Jewish community completely destroyed by the Nazis and their collaborators. When the dimensions of this catastrophe became clearer, we were overwhelmed with sorrow and emptiness.

And yet we didn't give up! We stood a little straighter. We picked up the pieces of our shattered lives and began the long uphill fight to build a new future. We studied languages and learned new trades. People clung to each other and fell in love.

There were weddings and great celebrations when babies were born . . . a declaration of life.

Soon I was well enough to think about my future. What a marvelous feeling that was. I had lost my childhood and young adulthood, but I was going to have a future. Over and over again, I repeated these words to myself, "I made it! I survived! I am safe! I am going to have a future!" These thoughts were so exhilarating that for awhile I could think of nothing else. But, in time, I did think of something else. I began to wonder about our future. Where would we go? Where would we live? Would we spend the rest of our lives in DP camps?

The fact that we had no place to go was devastating. Rebuilding our lives in Poland was not an option because we had nothing left there. To us, Poland was a vast graveyard. Besides, those who did go back were met with hatred and antisemitism.

Israel—a Jewish homeland—was but a dream to us. The British blockaded the shores of Palestine, and their patrols either sank or turned back boats full of Holocaust survivors to hopelessly crowded detention camps.

The United States had very strict immigration laws, and few of us could meet the requirements. Proper personal documents, blood relatives to sponsor us, and proof of good health were all impossible to come by. The indifference of the western world dealt the proverbial final blow to the battered psyche of the Jewish remnant, draining us of our last vestiges of energy. Later I learned that the Nazis found it much easier to enter the United States than did the survivors.

In the meantime Dr. Greenspan, my wonderful American doctor, brought me my first pair of new shoes. They were red, low-heeled and beautiful! He decided that it was time for me to go for a walk. The first few steps made me so heady with joy that I promptly passed out. Luckily, Dr. Greenspan caught me before I hit the ground. He carried me back inside, vowing that we would try again the next day. We did, and I succeeded. Soon I was walking daily and gaining weight.

By late summer 1945 it was clear to everyone that I was going to make it. It was then that Norbert decided to go to Poland in search of family and friends. He did find his niece Jadzia, who had been sheltered by a Christian family. But Jadzia's mother, Norbert's sister, had perished along with all the other members of Norbert's family.

While in Poland, Norbert tried to recover some money and jewelry which his family had given to Polish friends for safe-keeping. To his horror, he was literally chased out of Kraków. Some time later, the Poles massacred forty-two Jewish survivors in the town of Kielce, Poland. Although the war had ended, Polish antisemitism lived on. Norbert returned to Austria empty-handed.

For my seventeenth birthday Norbert gave me a small gold ring. The ring had a very special meaning because it once belonged to a young man who kept poison in its hollowed dome. The young man apparently intended to take his own life at the "right moment." A most defiant gesture at best.

Having a ring was, of course, forbidden in the camps, but this young man had tricked his captors by keeping his finger covered with a bloody bandage. Sadly, he never got the chance to take his own life. The Nazis beat him to it.

After he was killed his body, like those of other victims, was searched for valuables before being thrown into the crematoria. The searchers were prisoners assigned to this gruesome task. One of the *Sondercommandos,* as they were called, found the ring and managed to keep it. After the war was over, he gave the ring to Norbert because none of the victim's family had survived, and Norbert had been a friend of the victim.

Norbert, in turn, gave this special ring to me because he was concerned that I might not remember, that I might want to forget. Norbert believed that forgetting was dangerous. It was up to us, the survivors, to tell the world.

Norbert was an activist. Besides working for the Hebrew Immigrant Aid Society (HIAS), he quickly became involved in camp politics. He was always fighting for our community as well as for the rights of its individual members. When occupation forces wanted to return the abandoned farm on which Camp Hart had been built to the Austrian government, Norbert helped organize a protest rally. After a night of careful planning, he led us in a march on military headquarters. We were determined that we would not go back to Mauthausen. And we won! It was a great victory for us. After six years of captivity, after six years of being powerless, we were finally in the land of the living again. We finally had some control over our own fate.

Freedom brought other sensations as well. Having survived so much torment, I began to feel indestructible. In the beginning this feeling was no more than a nagging thought that I resisted and kept pushing away. Then, over time, the feeling crystallized until I came to believe that nothing would ever hurt me again. I had known every hurt, experienced every torment. I had seen it all and lost it all.

Feeling superhuman may be euphoric, but it doesn't last. As soon as we begin to care about others, we become vulnerable. And I cared. I watched the agony of survivors whose children were killed. I witnessed their grief, and I began to think about the enormity of this tragedy. Once again, I turned my thoughts into poetry.

What Else Was Lost?

One and a half million
Jewish children
and their children's
children . . .

Unthinkable numbers
But what hurts the most
Is the haunting thought
Of what else was lost
And how do we ever
Begin to mourn
The generations
Never to be born.

A leader, a hero,
An heir to a nation.
A builder. An artist.
A healer. A clown.

The cures undiscovered
The music unwritten
All the dreams undremt
Or shattered . . . or broken . . .
Unimagined treasure
The losses unmeasured
Unwept for
Unspoken.

In retrospect, I must have been mentally unbalanced. I cried a lot. I laughed a lot. I craved people, noise, and action. I was falling in and out of love at least once a week. I wanted only to live and enjoy life. But Norbert and Blanca had other plans for me. They insisted that I catch up on my education. And so with the help of tutors I studied a wide range of subjects, including English, French, math, art, philosophy, and music. I also worked with Norbert for the HIAS and joined the camp's theater group. There were not enough hours in the day for all I wanted to do.

But late at night, memories of the horrors I had lived through would come to me in nightmares. It was then that I would light some candles and write poetry to soothe myself back to sleep.

Stones Don't Weep

there was a time I knew for sure
that hell could be no worse
. . . a cesspool of humanity
my soul to immerse

but when the fog began to clear
I was bereft of pain and fear
and quite convinced that stones don't weep
I rocked myself to sleep

My nights were filled with horror, but my days were filled with surprises. I always looked forward to packages distributed by the United Nations Relief and Rehabilitation Administration (UNRRA). Once I found an evening gown in one of the packages. I wore it to my first New Year's Eve party.

We also found more useful clothing in the packages. And what we did not find, we made. We removed draperies from the windows of the nearby farmhouse and artfully transformed them into clothing. We sewed shirts, underwear, and even bathing suits from remnants of soft, silky parachutes which lay in the fields.

Someone gave me a piece of blue taffeta fabric just in time to make a dress for a very special occasion—a concert to which Dr. Greenspan had invited Blanca, Norbert and me. I had never been to a concert before! The anticipation was almost as delicious as the event itself.

Dr. Greenspan picked us up in a chauffeur-driven jeep. The ride was delightful and soon we arrived at a military installation. The concert was to be held outdoors, and the weather was fantastic. As far as the eye could see, the entire area was covered with soldiers sitting on the grass, laughing and relaxing. There were many flags and other decorations. The atmosphere was so festive that I became intoxicated with joy.

I could see the grandstand and hear the orchestra tuning up. Just a few feet from the orchestra, three high-ranking American officers sat in chairs. Everyone else was sitting on the ground. As we approached, the officers stood up, and Dr. Greenspan introduced us.

Then a most marvelous thing happened. The general smiled and with a grand gesture bowed to us. He said something to his companions and invited us to take their special seats. As the concert began, everyone settled down on the grass, except for the three survivors who sat in chairs. I felt reborn . . . worthy . . . human.

At some point I was reunited with Rena, my close friend from the Kraków Ghetto. Oh, what joy in finding her alive and near me! But even this happy occasion was marred. I learned that her father, whom I deeply loved, had been killed in Auschwitz.

It did not take long for Rena and me to resume our old friendship. Once more we laughed and cried together. We went to parties and dances. To the casual observer, we must have looked like two normal teenagers. When we heard that the Organization for Rehabilitation and Training (ORT) was offering courses on *How To Become A Cosmetician,* we immediately enrolled.

What a time we had making each other beautiful! Rena would spread a thick paste over my face and neck, and it would promptly harden. She would then go off in search of some concoction to remove the paste while I waited like a frozen mummy vowing to get even with her.

Also, in true teenage fashion, Rena covered for me when I got into trouble. For instance, there was that one afternoon when I went for a motorcycle ride with an American lieutenant. How I loved the excitement, the speed, the wind in my hair. But then disaster struck. As we neared a rather dangerous intersection in

Linz, we swerved to avoid an oncoming streetcar. We both spilled into the road, flying in different directions.

The young man later told me that, at first, he thought I was dead. Well, I was not dead. I was alive—bruised and bleeding but alive. I think that at that moment I feared Blanca more than death. She would have grounded me for a month had she found out what I had been up to. So Rena sneaked me into her room, cleaned me up, and gave me a change of clothes. Then she filed away this secret with my other misadventures.

After several months at Camp Hart we moved to Camp Bindermichel. Although, we now lived in a group of apartment houses, the accommodations were still very crowded and far from the freedom and normalcy we longed for. It was about this time that Rena met a young survivor named Marc. They fell in love and were soon married.

Of course, we all behaved and reacted differently. Just as Blanca worried about my recklessness, I worried about her sadness. Day after day I watched her sitting quietly for hours, listening to music with her eyes closed. Blanca needed quiet and solitude as much as I craved noise and action.

Then there was Henryk, a friend from the Kraków ghetto. Eighteen years old, the Holocaust had left him totally alone in the world except for Blanca, Norbert, and me. His experimentation with life took the form of exchanging goods on the black market. Needless to say, his activities were illegal and carefully watched. The military police or the Austrian authorities caught up with him at least once a week.

I had a soft spot in my heart for Henryk, first because I remembered him from the ghetto, but also because he had smuggled wonderful drinks to me when I had been at the hospital in Mauthausen. Now, at Camp Hart, he declared his eternal love for me.

Blanca and Norbert tried to protect and reform Henryk. But Henryk rarely used his charm and wit constructively. And so every time he got arrested, Norbert would bail him out and vouch for him. All the while I played the *femme fatale*, visiting him in jail and feeling very noble.

Just when I would begin to feel good about myself, even happy, something would pull at my gut and I would become sad, moody, and angry. Then came the doubts. I tried to fight them off, to ignore them. But the questions persisted. Why me? Why am I alive? Why not the others? Should I not feel guilty? Poetry provided a temporary escape.

My Western Wall

I built myself a Western Wall
Within the corner of my soul
And quite apart, deep in my heart
I lean against it to recall
Another time, another age
Another world of tears and rage
And there I often lay to rest
The agony within my breast.

Working for the HIAS, we were painfully aware of the many obstacles that displaced persons faced in trying to obtain visas to the outside world. Whenever we learned that a western country would issue entry permits to people with specific trades such as tailoring or farming, we became frustrated because few of us qualified.

Orphans—those eighteen and younger—usually qualified for adoption by Americans, Canadians, and others. Strange how birth dates came to haunt us again. In the ghettos and camps, the magic age for young people had been fourteen. Children under that age were killed. As a result, in the ghettos and camps, it was important to look older. Now eighteen became the magic number, and it was important to look younger. Although I qualified as an orphan, I would not leave without Norbert and Blanca.

Soon I became consumed with world news, especially news of Palestine. Day and night I dreamed of going there, where I could have a home among my own people. I wrote poetry to express my longing to live in Palestine.

Birthright

Was Jacob not my father's name
Did he not perish in the flame
Of prejudice—so that I might
Go home and claim my own birthright.

Did not his brothers share his fate
While nations fiddled in debate . . .
Did not their blood down rivers flow
Because they had no place to go . . .

There must not ever come to pass
Another time when those of us,
Whose children dwell in many lands.
Would face destruction at the hands
Of some demented "super" power;
There must not ever come an hour
When once again we'd stand alone . . .
Without a home to call our own.

I paint the sunset pink and gray,
A touch of blue . . . but when the day
Is done — I lie awake and stare
And cannot breathe for lack of air . . .

My hunger and my thirst to sate
I walk along the Zion-Gate . . .
And spread my wings in tender haste
The freedom of my soul to taste . . .

Yes, Jacob was my father's name
And he did perish in the flame
Of prejudice—so that I might
Go home and claim my own birthright.

Christian and family name: _Sonia_
Schreiber
Place and date of birth: _27.8.1928_
Krakow
Citizenship: _stateless_
Unmarried, married divorced, widowed: _____
unmarried
Profession: _officer_
Address: _Linz-Raimauer street 59_
Size: _165 cm_
Countenance: _round_
Eyes: _brown_
Hair: _d. fair_
Distinguishing marks: _none_

Linz the 10.9.46
Place and date of issue

Signature of officer in charge
officer of the passp. office

Nom et Prénom: _Sonia_
Schreiber
Lieu et date de naissance: _27.8.1928_
Krakow
Nationalité: _apatride_
État (célibataire, marié, divorcé, veuf[ve]): _____
fille
Profession: _fonctionnaire_
Domicile: _Linz. Rue de Raimauer 59_
Taille: _165 cm_
Visage: _rond_
Couleur des yeux: _brune_
Couleur des cheveux: _blonde_
Signes particuliers: _pas_

Linz. 10.9.46
Lieu et date de la délivrance

Signature du Service compétent
Adj. du bureau de passeports

One of Sonia's documents declaring her a "stateless" person.

While events in Palestine were making world news, events in Europe were also capturing world attention. In 1945 and 1946 the Allies put what was left of the Nazi leadership on trial in the city of Nuremberg, Germany. The former Nazi leaders were accused of crimes against humanity—murder, extermination, enslavement, deportation, and other inhumane acts committed against civilians before or during the war.

Norbert went to some of the Nuremberg trials and described them to us. To our disbelief, the Nazis pleaded innocent. They defended themselves by saying that they had only obeyed orders. The judges in Nuremberg sentenced twenty-five of the defendants to death by hanging; ninety-seven received prison terms of up to twenty-five years; and twenty were sentenced to life terms. Thirty-five were declared not guilty. Many top-ranking Nazi officials never stood trial. As the war ended Hitler committed suicide and others changed their identities and built new lives in Argentina, Australia, Canada, Germany, and the United States.

"And what of the other murderers?" we wondered. Thousands of SS men and women never stood trial. It seemed to us that the scales of justice collapsed under the weight of these crimes against humanity.

And they looked so normal, these murderers. Wouldn't it have been easier if they had looked like killers? But how does a killer look? How does a victim look? How does a survivor look?

Scars (and Stereotyping)

some of us carry visible scars
some bear the other kind,
both wrought to challenge sanity
and vanquish peace of mind

All during the time we were in the DP camps, Norbert had searched for Harry White, his uncle. Harry had left Poland before the war and settled somewhere near Boston, Massachusetts. Finally, in late 1947, Norbert met someone who told him that Uncle Harry and his family lived in Peabody, Massachusetts. Norbert wrote to Uncle Harry, who immediately agreed to sponsor us. Finally we qualified for entry into the United States.

Harry White was a kind and generous man. From the time Norbert first contacted him, he sent us caring letters which became our lifeline to the outside world. Uncle Harry worked quickly to sign the required affidavits which promised that Blanca, Norbert and I would not "become a burden to the United States government."

As we waited for our visas, I continued to have my own private battle with God. The following poem illustrates, in a most intimate way, this inner conflict and confirms the bargain I ultimately made with my faith.

85

Where Was Man?

You know I hated You oh Lord
I cursed Your blessed name
I needed help a sign a word
And there was no one else to blame

Because Your silence drove me mad
I climbed the walls and tore my hair
My lungs were spitting blood and yet
You wouldn't listen to my prayer

I called on You in torment wild
And desperately cursed Your name
Then I was nothing but a child
And there was no one else to blame

But now I feel God wasn't dead
And *where was man* I ask instead

On May 4, 1948, three years after the gates of Mauthausen had been opened by its inmates, Blanca, Norbert, and I arrived in New York. A few days later, Uncle Harry and his wonderful family welcomed us to Peabody. There, they helped us find an apartment as well as jobs in local factories. We were about to begin life again.

Blanca and Norbert in a D.P. Camp

9 *I Am Free*

I was nineteen years old when I began a new life in the United States. At that time, most Americans did not want to hear about the experiences of Holocaust survivors. (The word *Holocaust* was not even part of the vocabulary.) And most survivors did not have the will to talk about it, except among themselves. When some of us did break the silence and speak out, no one truly listened. Later, much later, some did listen, but very few heard. And so, in the beginning, I did not speak out. I concentrated, instead, on building a normal life.

But what constituted a "normal life" to a survivor of the Holocaust? The young people I met in 1948 came from another world. They had grown up with their families, lived in houses, slept in beds, eaten three meals a day, and gone to school. I, on the other hand, had been starved and brutalized. I dated a few young men, but these dates were always disastrous. We simply had nothing in common.

Then in 1949, I met Dr. Mark Weitz and fell in love with him. Mark was different from the young men I had dated. He was older and more mature. He had served with the medical corps during the war and had been wounded during the invasion of Normandy. As a result of his wartime experiences, Mark knew something of the agonies people are capable of inflicting upon each other. He was strong enough to endure my past and help me live in the present. We were married in 1950. Two years later our son was born. In 1955 we had twin daughters.

Blanca and Norbert were also busily rebuilding their lives. Their son was born in 1950 and a daughter in 1953. Life was not easy, but they managed. Norbert built a successful business.

Unfortunately, he had a serious heart condition, and his life ended in 1974. The loss was monumental.

During the 1950s and 1960s, I lived my life in much the same way as other American wives and mothers, at least to outward appearances. My inner world, however, differed dramatically. Over and over again, I heard my mother's final words to me, "Remember to tell the world." But how was I to do this? How was I to tell a world that did not want to listen? How was I to speak of the unspeakable—words that I myself did not want to hear? And so, as always, I turned to poetry. In 1965, I wrote a very long poem entitled "His Brother's Keeper." The following lines are excerpted from that poem:

From "His Brother's Keeper"

There is but a handful of survivors left
Who witnessed the nightmare in sorrow, bereft.
Must we tell again the details bizarre?
Must we show the wounds and tear at the scar?
The conscience of men compelled to awaken
For fear that the Martyr's Forest be forsaken.
Oh, what blasphemy to forget this slaughter,
To sop up the stains . . . dispose of the blotter.

When I first learned that historical revisionists were promoting books which claimed that the Holocaust had not taken place, I thought, "This must be a joke. How could seemingly intelligent people deny an event that had been so thoroughly documented by the murderers themselves?"

But I quickly realized that some people were listening to these pseudo-historians. The publications of the revisionists were often adorned with Ph.D.s and other professional degrees. Their materials began to appear in high school and college libraries and on the shelves of prestigious institutions.

When these events came to light, my own mind went into a spin—doing somersaults day and night. Nightmares that I had tucked away with great difficulty began to appear again. I hurt. I was angry. No! I was furious! I wanted to scream—to lash out. At first I tried to do this through my poetry.

Historical Distortionists

How can they say there was no Holocaust at all
How can they claim the flames were not for real
How can they steal my memories and violate
The very gate to my eternal grief . . .
They sent a thief to scrape the chimney walls,
To rape the halls and stomp upon the hallowed ground
Their evil lies resound beneath the ancient trees
Where bone and ashes can no longer rest in peace.

Later, in desperation, I consulted a lawyer. He seemed to understand my outrage and seriously suggested that I sue for defamation of soul. I felt a little better. I calmed down. Then, I began to think about the indignity of having to defend an undeniable truth, and I decided against legal action.

But I had to do something! I could not remain silent! "Well, I'll do it my way," I told myself. "After all, I do have a weapon. I am a survivor, an eyewitness, and it is about time that I speak out."

The timing for breaking my silence was quite favorable because in the late 70s there was a growing interest, even curiosity, about the Holocaust. First I spoke about my experiences at a local high school. Then, a young reporter asked for an interview. Her name was Harriet Tarnor Wacks.

Harriet wrote a sensitive and accurate article about my experiences. We quickly became friends. With her encouragement, I accepted more interviews and speaking engagements. Besides being a writer, Harriet is also a teacher. Salem State College soon asked us to teach a course about the Holocaust. Finally, in 1981, Harriet and I founded The Holocaust Center, Boston North, Inc. Its purpose was to promote Holocaust awareness by exploring the uniqueness of this historical event, and to apply its universal lessons to combat current racism, antisemitism, and bigotry. We still are deeply committed to this work.

About the same time, I became involved with the Facing History and Ourselves National Foundation. Participating in the Teacher Training Institutes widened my horizons considerably. Coordinating the annual survivors' workshops became a labor of love, and speaking in classrooms and adult education courses added a new dimension to my life.

Reliving the horrors was difficult, but the reactions of my audiences confirmed the rightness of what I was doing. I found that people cared, and their letters often encouraged me to explore my own feelings.

One day when I was reading my poetry in a classroom, a student said to me, "Your poetry is so gentle, don't you ever write anything vengeful or nasty? You know . . . "

"Yes, I know," I answered. "Quite recently. I wrote a very ugly poem. Just after a movie about the Holocaust was shown on German television, I read about a woman who didn't believe any of it. She questioned the very existence of death camps. She was convinced that the Holocaust was a Zionist plot. I was very angry. That night I wrote some hateful, ugly, terrible verses—but I never finished the poem."

Several days later, I received a letter from this student encouraging me to finish the poem. I did. In this poem, I refer to the fact that our horror did not end with death. The Nazis found ways to use the remains of their Jewish victims—human skin for lampshades, hair to stuff mattresses, fat for soap, and ashes for fertilizer.

The Holocaust Mini-Series
On TV in Germany

Ah, my pretty *Fraulein*
You are pale with disbelief
Did the picture on your "telly"
Turn your belly inside out?

See the lampshade on your lamp?
Now your hands are clammy-damp.
Hey, don't tell me to go to hell,
You know well that I'm your conscience —
Your Papa had none . . . and now he is gone.
To Argentina, you know.
So . . .

Go, get a breath of air,
But don't you dare choke,
When your nostrils fill with smoke . .
Its been there in the air,
All these years. You just didn't care,
To look, to smell
Oh well . . .

How does your garden grow?
Lush with fruit and flowers?
And what did *Frau* Bauers
Use to fertilize . . .
(That's a dirty trick)
You really look sick.

Ah, the Jews, the *Verdamte* Jews
How they come to haunt . . .
Just what do they want?
And you, you never even knew
A Jew . . .

Come on *Liebchen* don't despair,
Why do you stare at the ground?
What is it you found? There's a glimmer,
No, it isn't hope—you dope,
It's a gold tooth . . .

Your vision grows dimmer
And your mouth tastes sour,
You trample the flowers . . .
You slam the doors with force
And without grace . . .
Then you wash your face.
The water feels soothing, cool,
But like a fool you grope?
For a piece of soap . . .
And you scream . . .

Yet, in my dream,
I barely hear you moan,
. . . I have my own
Nightmares.

Because of the darkness and evil I have experienced, I often marvel at the resilience of the human spirit. What is it that forces us to bounce back after hitting bottom? My own reconnection with life occurred when I visited Israel. In that tiny corner of the world, for the first time in my life, I felt whole.

From "And There Was Light"

I want to shout praises so the world may hear,
Until mountains tremble through rock and debris,
For my heart is singing — Oh, so loud so clear:
I am free! I am free!

Yes, I saw the Children of Israel come home!
A spirit that nothing must ever impair;
Never more as outcasts to wander and roam
And die in despair . . .
In the still of the night you may hear a voice
That whispers a prayer of humble thanksgiving --
A Kadish . . . A tear . . . Then on to rejoice
And exalt the living.

My very own miracle happened to me
When my eyes beheld the blue skies above.
The meadows so green . . . and the emerald sea
As deep as the love
That seemed to surround me. Not a cloud in sight!
My heritage priceless in the face of time;
I drank of its beauty in wondrous delight —
Suspended . . . Sublime . . .

Epilogue
Going Back

During the early 1980s, my life was filled with remembering. Remembering became my job, my task, my obsession, my tormentor. Remembering was difficult, but I could do it. Then in 1986, a new challenge confronted me. I was invited to accompany Bernard Cardinal Law and a group of Catholics of Polish ancestry on a pilgrimage to Poland.

I was flattered and deeply grateful for the opportunity to further my efforts regarding Christian-Jewish relations. But I was also terrified. Remembering from a distance was one thing. Going back to the scene of the atrocities was another. For weeks I agonized over my decision. Finally, with the support of my husband, Blanca, and my children, I decided to go.

We arrived in Warsaw during a blinding rainstorm. The atmosphere was depressing, closed in. To me, Poland appeared to be a graveyard. And indeed, in some respects, it was. In the 1930s there had been almost 3.3 million Jewish men, women and children in Poland. That summer, 1986, there were fewer than 5,000. There were no rabbis in Poland, and most of the synagogues had been converted into museums or warehouses.

Since I had never lived in Warsaw, I did not experience much emotional trauma while I was there. But Kraków was a different matter. My body began trembling as soon as we entered the city.

This beautiful city of mine had once been home to a vibrant Jewish community of 60,000. In 1986 there were perhaps 200 Jewish people living in Kraków—all of them elderly. One Friday evening I visited Kraków's only remaining synagogue. That night my sadness turned to mourning and inconsolable grief. Once again, I questioned the sanity of my returning to Poland. I wrote:

95

40 Years Later

Why have I come to pierce this desolation
When fierce emotions like a dormant beast
Are tearing at my gut and feasting on my fear
Until I taste the bitterness of yesteryear.

Have I perhaps returned to find a reason
To help explain the ugliness and treason?
Did I not plan to challenge God's integrity
And make some sense of this insanity?

But . . . There is no special meaning to conceal
No pockets full of secrets to reveal
No thunder, no lightning, no great truth defined
Just a monstrous evil to torment my mind.

The Boston Globe, John Tlumacki

Standing in the Ashes of the crematoria at Birkenau. Sonia with Bernard Cardinal Law, Franciszek Cardinal Macharski and Leonard Zakim of the Anti Defamation League.

There were, of course, no answers to my questions, but still I continued on my journey back in time. In Kraków I stood by the ghetto wall on the Umschlag-Platz and remembered the night my mother had been taken from me. I prayed on the hill on which Plaszów had once stood and remembered the last time I had seen my father.

Our group journeyed to Auschwitz, and for the first time Jews and Christians prayed together there. I read some of my poetry and shared the following thoughts with my fellow pilgrims:

"For forty years, I tried to imagine coming back to this place of unspeakable horror. What would I feel? What would I think? How would I react standing upon the graveyard of our people? The questions are overwhelming. Do I evoke the names of my beloved parents—Janek and Adela? Do I recite the staggering numbers of my own loved ones, innocent men, women and children, condemned to death and slaughtered?"

I was haunted by the contradictions of this momentous experience. Standing upon the graveyard of my people was unreal and devastating, but weeping together amidst the ashes of the crematoria—the silent embrace between Jews and Christians—that was real.

The night of our visit to Auschwitz, I wrote:

Return to Auschwitz

This is unreal reality
A feeling empty and remote
I should devote eternity
To this colossal sense of loss

Instead I am confused, annoyed
I had prepared for other moods
For sadness, for insanity
But not this calm, horrific void

The hurt will surely come in time
With madness, anger, even tears
And I shall welcome these old friends
Whose touch I do no longer fear

Tonight my feelings are all wrong
I long to bring the sting of pain
Again to feel alive, aware
It is the numbness I can't bear

And yet I hope the sun will rise
Once more to warm humanity
To bind the wounds and heal the scars
Of this unreal reality

After Auschwitz I had one final memory to confront. I knew I could not leave Kraków without returning to my neighborhood, my street, and the house in which I had once lived. Before I knew it, I was embarking on this last stage in my journey.

As we drove down the streets of Kazimierz, I vowed to keep my emotions under control. We headed toward the river Wisla and stopped first at Dietla #1, the house in which Norbert had once lived. I imagined him playing soccer with his brothers, and then rushing off to meet Blanca. My heart beat a little faster as I looked up and down the street. It really had not changed very much. Suddenly I found myself in front of Dietla #21—my childhood address.

Although the little variety store was no longer there and the buildings were a bit neglected, everything seemed familiar. My heart pounding, I climbed two flights of stairs and knocked on the door of my family's apartment. When an elderly woman opened the door, I explained that I had once lived there and asked if I might come in.

Suddenly I was standing in my mother's kitchen. I looked at the small table against the wall and saw myself sitting there, doing homework. As if in a trance, I peeked into the family room and saw my parents at Shabbat dinner—candles burning, wine poured. And I could clearly hear my sister giggling on the sofa.

Then I moved to the balcony. Looking down into the courtyard, I could see myself as a little girl playing hopscotch beneath two trees. Those trees were very special because, when Blanca and I were born, my father had planted one for each of us.

Suddenly I came out of my trance and connected with the present. The trees, were they still here? All at once, I desperately needed to know the answer. But I also feared the answer. Had the trees vanished as my people had?

Hesitantly, I looked down into the courtyard. There, in that dark and dingy place, I saw one tree—its roots exposed, breaking through the cracked and crooked courtyard floor. One tree! One tree had survived. To me, it became a symbol of life.

When I returned home, I told Blanca about the tree. As always, my sister was most generous. With her usual good humor she declared, "It's your tree. I give it to you. I would never write a poem about it, but you will, won't you?"

I did.

The Tree of Life

There stands a tree, a lonely tree
Planted for me in a hostile land
Planted with love by my father's hand
The day I was born.

The roots gnarled and worn, broken and twisted
As if life ceased or never existed.

And yet, its limbs reach for the sun
And one (or two) with leaves
Green and tender, refused to surrender
And dared to survive. It *is* still alive.

I saw my tree, my birthday tree
Planted for me with my father's hands
It stands defiant, haunted, lonely
The last, the *only* . . . the tree of life.

This memoir is for my children,
for my sister's children,
and for their children
Don, Sandra, Andrea, Nachman, Tal, Roz, Dar
John, Elizabeth, Barbara, Stewart,
Ashley, Alissa, Abagail, Joshua, Rachael, Steve,
and for those yet to come.

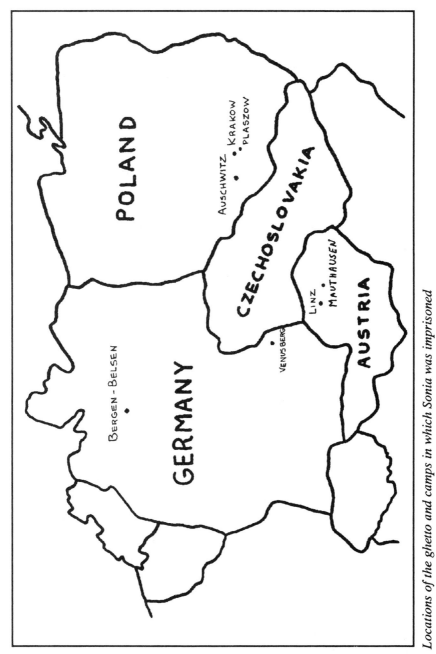

Locations of the ghetto and camps in which Sonia was imprisoned

Other Publications by
Facing History and Ourselves

Crimes Against Humanity and Civilization:
The Genocide of the Armenians
Between 1915 and 1923, it is estimated that the Young Turk
government of the Ottoman Empire systematically killed
more than 1.5 million of its Armenian citizens. This book
combines the latest scholarship on the Armenian Genocide
with an interdisciplinary approach to history, giving readers
the opportunity to concentrate on the choices and dilemmas
that individuals, groups, and nations faced before, during,
and after the genocide. While focusing on the Armenian
Genocide during World War I, the book considers the many
legacies of the Armenian Genocide including Turkish denial
and the struggle for the recognition of genocide as a "crime
against humanity."

Facing History and Ourselves:
Holocaust and Human Behavior
This resource book contains the essential materials needed
to incorporate the Facing History program into a school or
class. Its readings reflect the latest scholarship on the
Holocaust and include both primary sources and secondary
commentary that give clear examples of abuse of power,
violations of human rights, and unthinking obedience in
response to authority. The book provides sources and
methodology to explore prejudice, antisemitism, and dis-
crimination in our own lives and then investigates the failure of democracy and the rise of the Nazis in Germany and
the steps and events that led to the Holocaust. The final
chapter explores how positive participation in a democracy
can make a difference in achieving a society of tolerance and
justice.

Facing History and Ourselves:
The Jews of Poland

The Jews of Poland describes Jewish life in Eastern Europe before, during, and after the Holocaust. For centuries, Poland was home to about half of the Jews in the world. The book considers the ways they and their non-Jewish neighbors responded to questions of identity, membership, and difference at various times in their shared history. Students explore this history through excerpts of autobiographies, diaries, official documents, literary works, and other sources.

Race and Membership in American History:
The Eugenics Movement

At what point do differences become powerful social divisions? *Race and Membership in American History* explores this question by focusing on eugenics, a branch of "scientific" inquiry that sought to end social ills by ridding society of "inferior traits." In the early 20th century, racism and eugenics had worldwide appeal. In Nazi Germany they were used to justify racial policies that led to the Holocaust.

To order these and other resource materials from Facing History and Ourselves, please visit *www.facinghistory.org.*